Student Working Papers

THIRD CANADIAN EDITION

Accounting

Student Working Papers

NANCI LEE

THIRD CANADIAN EDITION

Accounting

NANCI LEE

AMERICAN RIVER COLLEGE

ELAINE HALES

GEORGIAN COLLEGE

Toronto

ISBN 0-13-042971-6

Senior Acquisitions Editor: Samantha Scully
Associate Editor: Rema Tatangelo
Production Editor: Söğüt Y. Güleç
Production Coordinator: Patricia Ciardullo

40 16

Printed and bound in the United States of America

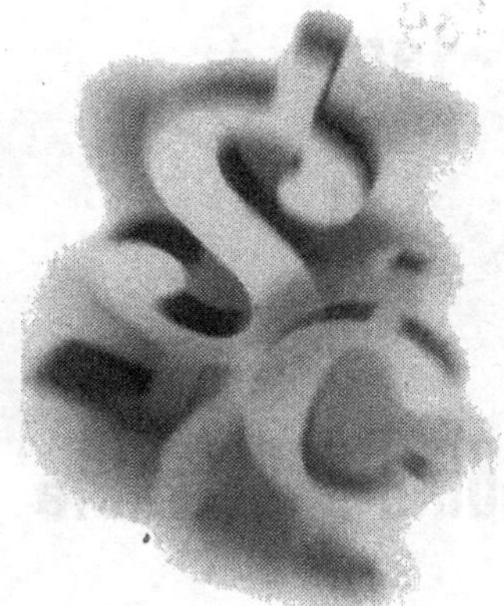

Contents

NAME:____________________________

CHAPTER 1

Starting a Business and the Balance Sheet

Vocabulary Review

1. ____________________
2. ____________________
3. ____________________
4. ____________________
5. ____________________
6. ____________________
7. ____________________
8. ____________________
9. ____________________
10. ____________________
11. ____________________
12. ____________________
13. ____________________
14. ____________________
15. ____________________
16. ____________________
17. ____________________
18. ____________________
19. ____________________
20. ____________________
21. ____________________
22. ____________________
23. ____________________
24. ____________________
25. ____________________
26. ____________________
27. ____________________
28. ____________________
29. ____________________
30. ____________________
31. ____________________
32. ____________________
33. ____________________
34. ____________________
35. ____________________
36. ____________________
37. ____________________
38. ____________________
39. ____________________
40. ____________________
41. ____________________
42. ____________________

NAME:____________________

Exercise 1.1

a. ____________________ f. ____________________
b. ____________________ g. ____________________
c. ____________________ h. ____________________
d. ____________________ i. ____________________
e. ____________________ j. ____________________

Exercise 1.2

a. ____________________ d. ____________________
b. ____________________ e. ____________________
c. ____________________ f. ____________________

Exercise 1.3

a. ____________________ f. ____________________
b. ____________________ g. ____________________
c. ____________________ h. ____________________
d. ____________________ i. ____________________
e. ____________________ j. ____________________

Exercise 1.4

a. ____________________ d. ____________________
b. ____________________ e. ____________________
c. ____________________

NAME: ____________________

Exercise 1.5

a. ____________________
b. ____________________
c. ____________________
d. ____________________
____
e. ____________________

Cash	________	Accounts Payable	________
Equipment	________	Capital	________
Furniture	________	Total Liabilities	
Total Assets	________	and Owner's Equity	________

Exercise 1.6

a. ____________________
b. ____________________
c. ____________________

Exercise 1.7

a. ____________________
b. ____________________
c. ____________________
d. ____________________

Exercise 1.8

a.	________	e.	________
b.	________	f.	________
c.	________	g.	________
d.	________	h.	________

NAME:____________________

Exercise 1.9

	Total Assets	Total Liabilities	Owner's Equity
a.	+	NC	+
b.			
c.			
d.			
e.			
f.			
g.			

Exercise 1.10

a. ____________________

____

b. ____________________

____

c. ____________________

____

____

NAME: ____________________

Problem 1.1

Instruction 1

	Cash	+ Grooming Supplies	+ Office Furniture	+ Office Equipment	+ Library	= Accounts Payable	+ Darlene Shear, Capital
a. Transaction							
New Balance							
b. Transaction							
New Balance							
c. Transaction							
New Balance							
d. Transaction							
New Balance							
e. Transaction							
New Balance							
f. Transaction							
New Balance							
g. Transaction							
New Balance							

Instruction 2

Cash	________	Accounts Payable	________
Grooming Supplies	________	Darlene Shear, Capital	________
Office Furniture	________		
Office Equipment	________		
Library	________	Total Liabilities and Owner's Equity	________
Total Assets	________		

NAME:____________________

Problem 1.2

Instruction 1

____

____

____

Instruction 2

Make sure that you check each item "a" through "h" to ensure that you have accurately prepared the balance sheet as directed in Instruction 1.

NAME:____________________

Problem 1.3

Instruction 1

	Cash	+	Library	+	Equipment	+	Furniture	=	Accounts Payable	+	Brian Jardin, Capital
a. Transaction											
New Balance											
b. Transaction											
New Balance											
c. Transaction											
New Balance											
d. Transaction											
New Balance											
e. Transaction											
New Balance											
f. Transaction											
New Balance											
g. Transaction											
New Balance											

Instruction 2

Cash	__________	Accounts Payable	__________
Library	__________	Brian Jardin, Capital	__________
Equipment	__________		
Furniture	__________		
Total Assets	__________	Total Liabilities and Owner's Equity	__________

NAME:________________________

Problem 1.3 *(continued)*

Instruction 3

____

____

____

NAME:__________________________

Problem 1.4

Instruction 1

a. Cash ________________

Equipment ________________

Exercise Mats ________________

Stereo System ________________

Furniture ________________

Lighting Fixtures ________________

b. Total Assets ________________

c. Accounts Payable ________________________________

d. Capital ________________________________

NAME:________________________

Problem 1.4 *(continued)*

Instruction 2

NAME:____________________

Problem 1.5

Instruction 1

	Cash	+	Supplies	+	Equipment	+	Furniture	=	Accounts Payable	+	Pete Fredericks, Capital
a. Transaction											
New Balance											
b. Transaction											
New Balance											
c. Transaction											
New Balance											
d. Transaction											
New Balance											
e. Transaction											
New Balance											
f. Transaction											
New Balance											

Instruction 2

Cash	____________	Accounts Payable	____________
Supplies	____________	Pete Fredericks, Capital	____________
Equipment	____________		
Furniture	____________	Total Liabilities and Owner's Equity	____________
Total Assets	____________		

NAME:_______________________

Problem 1.5 *(continued)*

Instruction 3

____

____

____

NAME:______________________

CHAPTER 2

Profitability and the Income Statement

Vocabulary Review

1. ______________________
2. ______________________
3. ______________________
4. ______________________
5. ______________________
6. ______________________
7. ______________________
8. ______________________
9. ______________________
10. ______________________
11. ______________________
12. ______________________
13. ______________________
14. ______________________
15. ______________________
16. ______________________
17. ______________________
18. ______________________
19. ______________________
20. ______________________
21. ______________________
22. ______________________
23. ______________________
24. ______________________
25. ______________________
26. ______________________
27. ______________________
28. ______________________

NAME:____________________

Exercise 2.1

a. ____________________
b. ____________________
c. ____________________
d. ____________________
e. ____________________
f. ____________________
g. ____________________
h. ____________________
i. ____________________
j. ____________________
k. ____________________
l. ____________________
m. ____________________
n. ____________________

Exercise 2.2

Instruction 1

Cash	________	Accounts Payable	________
Accounts Receivable	________	Capital	________
Equipment	________	Revenue	________
		Subtotal	________
		Less: Expenses	________
		Drawing	________
Total Assets	________	Total	________

____

Instruction 2

a. ____________________
b. ____________________
c. ____________________
d. ____________________
____
e. ____________________
f. ____________________
g. ____________________
h. ____________________
i. ____________________

NAME:____________________

Exercise 2.2 *(continued)*

Instruction 3

Revenue __________

Expenses __________

Net Income __________

Instruction 4

Ending Capital ____________________

Exercise 2.3

a. ____________________

____

b. ____________________

c. ____________________

d. ____________________

____

e. ____________________

f. ____________________

g. ____________________

NAME:______________________________

Exercise 2.4

Instruction 1

____

____

____

NAME: ______________________

Exercise 2.5

____

____

____

NAME:________________

Exercise 2.6

a. ________________

____

b. ________________

____

c. ________________

____

d. ________________

____

e. ________________

____

f. ________________

____

g. ________________

____

h. ________________

____

i. ________________

____

j. ________________

____

k. ________________

____

NAME:______________________

Exercise 2.7

Instruction 1

____

____

____

NAME:___________________________

Exercise 2.8

Exercise 2.9

NAME: ______________________

Exercise 2.10

a. Capital, February 1

Deduct: Net Loss

Drawing

Capital, February 28

b.

c.

d.

e.

NAME:______________________

Exercise 2.11

Owner's Equity, January 31	
Owner's Equity, January 1	
Increase in Owner's Equity	

	Net Income or Net Loss?	Calculation	Amount of Net Income or Net Loss
a.			
b.			
c.			

NAME: ____________________

Problem 2.1

Instruction 1

		Cash	+	Accounts Receivable	+	Supplies	+	Furniture	+	Equipment	=	Accounts Payable	+	Mar Capital	+	Revenue	–	Expenses	–	Drawing
a.	Transaction																			
	New Balance																			
b.	Transaction																			
	New Balance																			
c.	Transaction																			
	New Balance																			
d.	Transaction																			
	New Balance																			
e.	Transaction																			
	New Balance																			
f.	Transaction																			
	New Balance																			
g.	Transaction																			
	New Balance																			
h.	Transaction																			
	New Balance																			
i.	Transaction																			
	New Balance																			
j.	Transaction																			
	New Balance																			

NAME: ______________________

Problem 2.1 *(continued)*

Instruction 1

	Cash	+	Accounts Receivable	+	Supplies	+	Furniture	+	Equipment	=	Accounts Payable	+	Mar Capital	+	Revenue	–	Expenses	–	Drawing
Balance Fwd.																			
k. Transaction																			
New Balance																			
l. Transaction																			
New Balance																			
m. Transaction																			
New Balance																			

NAME:____________________

Problem 2.1 *(continued)*

Instruction 2

Cash	________	Accounts Payable	________
Accounts Receivable	________	Capital	________
Supplies	________	Revenue	________
Furniture	________	Subtotal	________
Equipment	________	Deduct: Expenses	________
		Drawing	________
Total Assets	________	Total Liabilities and Owner's Equity	________

Instruction 3

Instruction 4

NAME: ______________________________

Problem 2.2

Instruction 1

Instruction 2

NAME: ____________________

Problem 2.3

Instruction 1

		Cash	+	Accounts Receivable	+	Supplies	+	Furniture	+	Equipment	=	Accounts Payable	+	Capital	+	Revenue	–	Expenses	–	Drawing
a.	Transaction																			
	New Balance																			
b.	Transaction																			
	New Balance																			
c.	Transaction																			
	New Balance																			
d.	Transaction																			
	New Balance																			
e.	Transaction																			
	New Balance																			
f.	Transaction																			
	New Balance																			
g.	Transaction																			
	New Balance																			
h.	Transaction																			
	New Balance																			
i.	Transaction																			
	New Balance																			
j.	Transaction																			
	New Balance																			

NAME: ____________________

Problem 2.3 *(continued)*

Instruction 1

	Cash	+	Accounts Receivable	+	Supplies	+	Furniture	+	Equipment	=	Accounts Payable	+	Capital	+	Revenue	−	Expenses	−	Drawing
Balance Fwd.																			
k. Transaction																			
New Balance																			
l. Transaction																			
New Balance																			
m. Transaction																			
New Balance																			
n. Transaction																			
New Balance																			
o. Transaction																			
New Balance																			
p. Transaction																			
New Balance																			

NAME: ____________________

Problem 2.3 *(continued)*

Instruction 2

Cash	________	Accounts Payable	________
Accounts Receivable	________	Capital	________
Supplies	________	Revenue	________
Furniture	________	Subtotal	________
Equipment	________	Deduct: Expenses	________
		Drawing	________
Total Assets	________	Total Liabilities and Owner's Equity	________

Instruction 3

____

____

____

NAME:________________________

Problem 2.3 *(continued)*

Instruction 4

____

____

____

NAME:____________________

Problem 2.4

Instruction 1

Instruction 2

NAME:______________________________

Problem 2.4 *(continued)*

Instruction 3

____

____

____

NAME:________________________

Problem 2.5

____

____

____

NAME:____________________

Problem 2.6

Example: Overstated (Revenue is higher than it should be)

a. ____________________

b. ____________________

c. ____________________

d. ____________________

e. ____________________

f. ____________________

g. ____________________

NAME:______________________________

CHAPTER 3

Understanding Debits and Credits and the Trial Balance

Vocabulary Review

1. ______________________________
2. ______________________________
3. ______________________________
4. ______________________________
5. ______________________________
6. ______________________________
7. ______________________________
8. ______________________________
9. ______________________________
10. ______________________________
11. ______________________________
12. ______________________________
13. ______________________________
14. ______________________________
15. ______________________________
16. ______________________________
17. ______________________________
18. ______________________________
19. ______________________________
20. ______________________________

NAME:____________________________

Exercise 3.1

0. **Cash**

Debit	Credit
+	−

1. **Owner, Capital**

Debit	Credit

2. **Accounts Receivable**

Debit	Credit

3. **Notes Payable**

Debit	Credit

4. **Rent Expense**

Debit	Credit

5. **Commission Revenue**

Debit	Credit

6. **Owner, Drawing**

Debit	Credit

7. **Supplies**

Debit	Credit

8. **Accounts Payable**

Debit	Credit

9. **Rental Revenue**

Debit	Credit

10. **Utilities Expense**

Debit	Credit

NAME:____________________

Exercise 3.2

Instruction A

	Would Cause an Increase	Would Cause an Decrease
1. a credit to Accounts Receivable		
2. a debit to Drawing		
3. a debit to Accounts Payable		
4. a debit to Interest Expense		
5. a credit to Capital		
6. a credit to Cash		
7. a debit to Notes Receivable		
8. a credit to Accounts Payable		
9. a debit to Accounts Receivable		
10. a credit to Revenue		
11. a debit to Cash		
12. a debit to Advertising Expense		
13. a credit to Notes Receivable		
14. a debit to Capital		
15. a debit to Mortgage Payable		

NAME:________________________

Exercise 3.2 *(continued)*

Instruction B

	Normal Debit Balance	Normal Credit Balance
16. Accounts Payable	__________	__________
17. Capital	__________	__________
18. Furniture	__________	__________
19. Drawing	__________	__________
20. Wages Expense	__________	__________
21. Cash	__________	__________
22. Revenue from Sales	__________	__________
23. Taxes Payable	__________	__________
24. Supplies	__________	__________
25. Equipment	__________	__________
26. Gas and Oil Expense	__________	__________
27. Commissions Revenue	__________	__________
28. Accounts Receivable	__________	__________
29. Automobile	__________	__________
30. Advertising Expense	__________	__________

NAME:____________________

Exercise 3.3

Cash — 101

	Debit		Credit
a)	15,000	b)	360
d)	1,100	c)	1,720
l)	250	e)	640
n)	780	h)	830
		i)	1,940
		j)	115
		k)	4,000
		m)	830
		q)	620
		r)	130

Accounts Receivable — 110

	Debit		Credit
g)	950	n)	780

Supplies — 115

	Debit		Credit
q)	620		

Furniture — 120

	Debit		Credit
c)	5,100		
k)	4,000		

Accounts Payable — 210

	Debit		Credit
h)	830	c)	3,380
		f)	155

Notes Payable — 215

	Debit		Credit
		p)	28,000

Sandra Samson, Capital — 301

	Debit		Credit
		a)	15,000
		o)	2,200

Sandra Samson, Drawing — 305

	Debit		Credit
m)	830		

Dental Revenue — 401

	Debit		Credit
		d)	1,100
		g)	950
		l)	250

Salary Expense — 601

	Debit		Credit
b)	360		
i)	1,940		

NAME: ____________________

Exercise 3.3 *(continued)*

Library		125
o)	2,200	

Automobile		140
p)	28,000	

Advertising Expense		615
f)	155	

Rent Expense		605
e)	640	

Utilities Expense		610
j)	115	

Interest Expense		620
r)	130	

____

____

____

NAME:______________________

Exercise 3.4

a. Original investment by owner

b. ______________________

c. ______________________

____

d. ______________________

e. ______________________

f. ______________________

g. ______________________

h. ______________________

i. ______________________

j. ______________________

k. ______________________

l. ______________________

m. ______________________

n. ______________________

o. ______________________

p. ______________________

____

q. ______________________

r. ______________________

NAME:________________________

Exercise 3.5

NAME:______________________

Exercise 3.6

0. **Cash** 100 — Debit: 10,000
   Land 120 — Debit: 75,000
   Jack Feder, Capital 301 — Credit: 85,000

a. **Office Equipment** 115 | **Cash** 100 | **Notes Payable** 210

b. **Advertising Expense** 625 | **Cash** 100

c. **Supplies** 109 | **Cash** 100 | **Accounts Payable** 205

d. **Rent Expense** 635 | **Cash** 100

e. **Cash** 100 | **Notes Payable** 210

f.

g.

h.

i.

NAME:____________________

Exercise 3.6 *(continued)*

j.

k.

l.

m.

n.

o.

p.

Exercise 3.7

a.

b.

c.

d.

e.

f.

g.

h.

i.

j.

NAME:________________________

Exercise 3.8

	Revenue	Expense
a.		
b.		
c.		
d.		
e.		

Exercise 3.9

	Will Trial Balance totals be unequal?	Which column will be larger?	How much larger will it be?
Example:	Yes	Credit	$ 50
a.			
b.			
c.			
d.			
e.			
f.			
g.			
h.			
i.			
j.			

NAME:______________________

Problem 3.1

Instruction 1

a. ______________________

b. ______________________

c. ______________________

____

d. ______________________

e. ______________________

f. ______________________

g. ______________________

h. ______________________

i. ______________________

j. ______________________

k. ______________________

l. ______________________

m. ______________________

n. ______________________

o. ______________________

p. ______________________

q. ______________________

r. ______________________

s. ______________________

____

t. ______________________

u. ______________________

v. ______________________

NAME:________________________

Problem 3.1 *(continued)*

Instructions 2 and 3

____

____

____

NAME:__________________________

Problem 3.1 *(continued)*

Instruction 4

NAME:____________________

Problem 3.1 *(continued)*

Instruction 5

NAME:______________________

Problem 3.2

Instructions 1, 2 and 3

Cash	100

Accounts Receivable	110

Medical Supplies	120

Office Supplies	130

Equipment	140

Accounts Payable	210

Notes Payable	220

Shawn O'Brien, Capital	310

NAME:____________________

Problem 3.2 *(continued)*

Instructions 1, 2 and 3

Shawn O'Brien, Drawing 320

Revenue 410

Rent Expense 610

Salary Expense 620

Utilities Expense 630

Insurance Expense 650

NAME:______________________________

Problem 3.2 *(continued)*

Instruction 4

____

____

____

NAME:________________________

Problem 3.3

Instructions 1, 2, 3 and 4

Cash **101**

Debit	Credit
Balance 10,500	

Accounts Receivable **110**

Debit	Credit
Balance 4,400	

Office Supplies **115**

Debit	Credit
Balance 970	

Delivery Van **120**

Debit	Credit
Balance 25,000	

Computer Equipment **130**

Debit	Credit
Balance 7,500	

Office Equipment **140**

Debit	Credit
Balance 11,600	

Accounts Payable **210**

Debit	Credit
	Balance 7,500

NAME:______________________________

Problem 3.3 *(continued)*

Instructions 1, 2, 3 and 4

Notes Payable 215

	Balance 33,500

Pierre Legault, Capital 301

	Balance 18,970

Pierre Legault, Drawing 310

Floral Revenue 401

Rent Expense 601

Utilities Expense 605

Advertising Expense 610

Interest Expense 615

Gas & Oil Expense 620

Repairs Expense 625

Insurance Expense 630

Salaries Expense 640

NAME:________________________

Problem 3.3 *(continued)*

Instruction 5

NAME:________________________

Problem 3.3 *(continued)*

Instruction 6

NAME:________________________

Problem 3.3 *(continued)*

Instruction 7

NAME:__________________________

Problem 3.4

Instructions 1, 2 and 3

Cash 100

+	–
Balance 2,000	

Accounts Receivable 105

+	–
Balance 1,800	

Grooming Supplies 110

+	–
Balance 600	

Grooming Equipment 115

+	–
Balance 5,700	

Office Furniture 120

+	–
Balance 4,900	

Van 125

+	–
Balance 18,000	

Accounts Payable 201

–	+
	Balance 3,000

NAME:_______________

Problem 3.4 *(continued)*

Instructions 1, 2 and 3

Notes Payable 210

−	+
	Balance 12,000

Frances Schultz, Capital 305

−	+
	Balance 18,000

Frances Schultz, Drawing 310

+	−

Grooming Revenue 401

−	+

Rent Expense 605

+	−

Utilities Expense 610

+	−

Insurance Expense 612

+	−

Advertising Expense 615

+	−

Repairs Expense 620

+	−

Gas & Oil Expense 625

+	−

Interest Expense 630

+	−

NAME:________________________

Problem 3.4 *(continued)*

Instruction 4

NAME:____________________

Problem 3.4 *(continued)*

Instruction 5

Instruction 6

NAME:____________________

Problem 3.4 *(continued)*

Instruction 7

____

____

____

NAME:______________________________

Problem 3.5

Instruction 1

Cash 101

a)	25,000	b)	4,000
i)	450	d)	5,000
m)	1,050	e)	3,200
q)	520	f)	800
v)	1,500	g)	1,200
		k)	150
		l)	370
		o)	2,500
		r)	1,000
		s)	290
		t)	370
		u)	900

Accounts Receivable 120

j)	520	q)	520
p)	750		

Supplies 130

c)	4,500		
e)	3,200		

Equipment 140

b)	10,000		
d)	8,000		

Accounts Payable 210

o)	2,500	c)	4,500
s)	290	h)	600
		n)	290

Notes Payable 220

r)	1,000	b)	6,000
		d)	3,000

Maria Fore, Capital 310

		a)	25,000

Maria Fore, Drawing 320

u)	900		

NAME:____________________________

Problem 3.5 *(continued)*

Instruction 1

Repair Revenue			410
		i)	450
		j)	520
		m)	1,050
		p)	750
		v)	1,500

Rent Expense			610
f)	800		

Utilities Expense			620
k)	150		

Salary Expense			630
l)	370		
t)	370		

Repair Parts Expense			640
n)	290		

Advertising Expense			650
g)	1,200		
h)	600		

NAME:________________________

Problem 3.5 *(continued)*

Instruction 2

NAME:______________________

Problem 3.6

Instruction 1

	Will error affect Net Income?	Will Net Income be overstated?	Will Net Income be understated?
a.			
b.			
c.			
d.			
e.			
f.			
g.			

Instruction 2

Net income before corrections	$7,200

NAME:______________________

CHAPTER 4

The General Journal and the General Ledger

Vocabulary Review

1. ______________________
2. ______________________
3. ______________________
4. ______________________
5. ______________________
6. ______________________
7. ______________________
8. ______________________
9. ______________________
10. ______________________
11. ______________________
12. ______________________
13. ______________________
14. ______________________
15. ______________________
16. ______________________
17. ______________________
18. ______________________
19. ______________________
20. ______________________
21. ______________________
22. ______________________
23. ______________________
24. ______________________
25. ______________________
26. ______________________
27. ______________________
28. ______________________

NAME:______________________

Exercise 4.1

Instructions 1, 2, 3, 4 and 5

GENERAL LEDGER

CASH — ACCT. NO. 101

Date		Explanation	Post. Ref.	Debit	Credit	Balance

ACCOUNTS RECEIVABLE — ACCT. NO. 110

Date		Explanation	Post. Ref.	Debit	Credit	Balance

SUPPLIES — ACCT. NO. 120

Date		Explanation	Post. Ref.	Debit	Credit	Balance

NAME:________________________

Exercise 4.1 *(continued)*

Instructions 1, 2, 3, 4 and 5

EQUIPMENT ACCT. NO. 130

Date		Explanation	Post. Ref.	Debit	Credit	Balance

ACCOUNTS PAYABLE ACCT. NO. 210

Date		Explanation	Post. Ref.	Debit	Credit	Balance

Y. GOLDSTEIN, CAPITAL ACCT. NO. 310

Date		Explanation	Post. Ref.	Debit	Credit	Balance

Y. GOLDSTEIN, DRAWING ACCT. NO. 320

Date		Explanation	Post. Ref.	Debit	Credit	Balance

REVENUE ACCT. NO. 405

Date		Explanation	Post. Ref.	Debit	Credit	Balance

INSURANCE EXPENSE ACCT. NO. 610

Date		Explanation	Post. Ref.	Debit	Credit	Balance

UTILITIES EXPENSE ACCT. NO. 620

Date		Explanation	Post. Ref.	Debit	Credit	Balance

NAME:______________________

Exercise 4.1 *(continued)*

Instructions 1, 2, 3, 4 and 5

ADVERTISING EXPENSE — ACCT. NO. 630

Date		Explanation	Post. Ref.	Debit	Credit	Balance

Exercise 4.2

GENERAL LEDGER

CASH — ACCT. NO. 101

Date		Explanation	Post. Ref.	Debit	Credit	Balance

ACCOUNTS RECEIVABLE — ACCT. NO. 110

Date		Explanation	Post. Ref.	Debit	Credit	Balance

SUPPLIES — ACCT. NO. 120

Date		Explanation	Post. Ref.	Debit	Credit	Balance

NAME:________________________

Exercise 4.2 *(continued)*

Instructions 1, 2, 3, 4 and 5

EQUIPMENT — ACCT. NO. 130

Date		Explanation	Post. Ref.	Debit	Credit	Balance

ACCOUNTS PAYABLE — ACCT. NO. 210

Date		Explanation	Post. Ref.	Debit	Credit	Balance

PAT O'HENRY, CAPITAL — ACCT. NO. 310

Date		Explanation	Post. Ref.	Debit	Credit	Balance

PAT O'HENRY, DRAWING — ACCT. NO. 320

Date		Explanation	Post. Ref.	Debit	Credit	Balance

REVENUE FROM SERVICES — ACCT. NO. 410

Date		Explanation	Post. Ref.	Debit	Credit	Balance

UTILITIES EXPENSE — ACCT. NO. 610

Date		Explanation	Post. Ref.	Debit	Credit	Balance

NAME:______________________

Exercise 4.3

Instruction 1

GENERAL LEDGER

CASH **ACCT. NO. 101**

Date		Explanation	Post. Ref.	Debit	Credit	Balance
20XX May	31	Balance Forward	✓			2000—
June	1		GJ20	50—		
	7		GJ20	375—		
	8		GJ20		130—	
	10		GJ20		400—	
	14		GJ20	400—		
	15		GJ21		500—	
	15		GJ21		300—	
	16		GJ21		140—	
	18		GJ21		400—	
	25		GJ22		300—	
	28		GJ22	520—		
	29		GJ22		85—	
	30		GJ22	100—		

ACCOUNTS RECEIVABLE **ACCT. NO. 105**

Date		Explanation	Post. Ref.	Debit	Credit	Balance
20XX May	31	Balance Forward	✓			500—
June	1		GJ20		50—	
	21		GJ21	250—		
	30		GJ22		100—	

NAME: ____________________

Exercise 4.3 *(continued)*

Instruction 1

SUPPLIES — ACCT. NO. 108

Date 20XX		Explanation	Post. Ref.	Debit	Credit	Balance
May	31	Balance Forward	✓			400—
June	8		GJ20	130—		

EQUIPMENT — ACCT. NO. 110

Date 20XX		Explanation	Post. Ref.	Debit	Credit	Balance
May	31	Balance Forward	✓			5000—

ACCOUNTS PAYABLE — ACCT. NO. 205

Date 20XX		Explanation	Post. Ref.	Debit	Credit	Balance
May	31	Balance Forward	✓			2000—
June	10		GJ20	400—		
	18		GJ21	400—		

BUCK JENSEN, CAPITAL — ACCT. NO. 310

Date 20XX		Explanation	Post. Ref.	Debit	Credit	Balance
May	31	Balance Forward	✓			5900—

BUCK JENSEN, DRAWING — ACCT. NO. 311

Date 20XX		Explanation	Post. Ref.	Debit	Credit	Balance
June	15		GJ21	500—		
	25		GJ22	300—		

GUIDE REVENUE — ACCT. NO. 401

Date 20XX		Explanation	Post. Ref.	Debit	Credit	Balance
June	7		GJ20		375—	
	14		GJ20		400—	
	21		GJ21		250—	
	28		GJ22		520—	

NAME:_______________________

Exercise 4.3 *(continued)*

Instruction 1

STABLE EXPENSE — **ACCT. NO. 610**

Date		Explanation	Post. Ref.	Debit	Credit	Balance
20XX June	16		GJ21	140 —		
	29		GJ22	85 —		

RENT EXPENSE — **ACCT. NO. 620**

Date		Explanation	Post. Ref.	Debit	Credit	Balance
20XX June	15		GJ21	300 —		

Instruction 2

____

____

____

NAME:____________________

Exercise 4.4

GENERAL JOURNAL			PAGE NO.	
Date	Description	Post. Ref.	Debit	Credit

NAME:________________________

Exercise 4.4 *(continued)*

GENERAL JOURNAL			PAGE NO.	
Date	Description	Post. Ref.	Debit	Credit

NAME: ____________________

Exercise 4.4 *(continued)*

GENERAL JOURNAL PAGE NO.

Date		Description	Post. Ref.	Debit	Credit

NAME:____________________

Exercise 4.5

	Number	Sum of the digits	Evenly divisible by 9?
1.	306.42		
2.	7,234.12		
3.	46,728		
4.	416,732.85		
5.	8,334.00		
6.	3,939.93		
7.	423		
8.	5.721		
9.	46,901.30		
10.	74,615.91		

Exercise 4.6

	Number as it should be recorded	Number as it is actually recorded	Difference	Divide difference by 9
0.	873	837	36	$36 \div 9 = 4$
1.	749	794		
2.	105.20	1,052.00		
3.	37,654	37,645		
4.	10.97	1.097		
5.	52	25		
6.	1.28	2.18		
7.	204	2,040		
8.	7.39	7.93		
9.	40,639	46,039		
10.	10,828	10,288		

NAME:____________________

Exercise 4.7

	Debit column	Credit column	Difference	Sum of the digits	Is error likely to be a slide or transposition (yes or no)
0.	17,604.21	18,522.48	918.27	27	yes
1.	70,732	70,822			
2.	10,450	10,498			
3.	21,732	22,722			
4.	106,549	105,326			
5.	185,410	176,320			

Exercise 4.8

	Will Trial Balance totals be unequal?	If so, by how much?	Which column will be larger?
a.			
b.			
c.			
d.			
e.			
f.			
g.			
h.			

NAME:________________________

Exercise 4.9

	Total Revenue	Total Expenses	Total Net Income
Example:	Not affected	Overstated	Understated
a.			
b.			
c.			
d.			
e.			
f.			
g.			
h.			

NAME:_______________________

Problem 4.1

Instruction 1

GENERAL JOURNAL			PAGE NO.	
Date	Description	Post. Ref.	Debit	Credit

NAME:________________________

Problem 4.1 *(continued)*

Instruction 1

GENERAL JOURNAL			PAGE NO.	
Date	Description	Post. Ref.	Debit	Credit

NAME:____________________

Problem 4.1 *(continued)*

Instruction 1

GENERAL JOURNAL		PAGE NO.		
Date	Description	Post. Ref.	Debit	Credit

NAME:____________________

Problem 4.1 *(continued)*

Instruction 2

GENERAL LEDGER

CASH **ACCT. NO. 101**

Date		Explanation	Post. Ref.	Debit	Credit	Balance

ACCOUNTS RECEIVABLE **ACCT. NO. 105**

Date		Explanation	Post. Ref.	Debit	Credit	Balance

SUPPLIES **ACCT. NO. 110**

Date		Explanation	Post. Ref.	Debit	Credit	Balance

NAME:________________________

Problem 4.1 *(continued)*

Instruction 2

EQUIPMENT — **ACCT. NO. 115**

Date		Explanation	Post. Ref.	Debit	Credit	Balance

AIRPLANE — **ACCT. NO. 120**

Date		Explanation	Post. Ref.	Debit	Credit	Balance

ACCOUNTS PAYABLE — **ACCT. NO. 220**

Date		Explanation	Post. Ref.	Debit	Credit	Balance

NOTES PAYABLE — **ACCT. NO. 230**

Date		Explanation	Post. Ref.	Debit	Credit	Balance

DIZZY DAWSON, CAPITAL — **ACCT. NO. 301**

Date		Explanation	Post. Ref.	Debit	Credit	Balance

DIZZY DAWSON, DRAWING — **ACCT. NO. 310**

Date		Explanation	Post. Ref.	Debit	Credit	Balance

NAME:____________________

Problem 4.1 *(continued)*

Instruction 2

FLYING REVENUE ACCT. NO. 401

Date		Explanation	Post. Ref.	Debit	Credit	Balance

REPAIRS EXPENSE ACCT. NO. 610

Date		Explanation	Post. Ref.	Debit	Credit	Balance

INSURANCE EXPENSE ACCT. NO. 615

Date		Explanation	Post. Ref.	Debit	Credit	Balance

ADVERTISING EXPENSE ACCT. NO. 620

Date		Explanation	Post. Ref.	Debit	Credit	Balance

FUEL EXPENSE ACCT. NO. 630

Date		Explanation	Post. Ref.	Debit	Credit	Balance

RENT EXPENSE ACCT. NO. 640

Date		Explanation	Post. Ref.	Debit	Credit	Balance

INTEREST EXPENSE ACCT. NO. 650

Date		Explanation	Post. Ref.	Debit	Credit	Balance

NAME:____________________________

Problem 4.1 *(continued)*

Instruction 3

____

____

____

NAME:____________________

Problem 4.1 *(continued)*

Instruction 4

____

____

____

NAME:__________________________

Problem 4.1 *(continued)*

Instruction 5

NAME:________________________

Problem 4.2

Instructions 1 and 3

GENERAL LEDGER

CASH **ACCT. NO. 101**

Date		Explanation	Post. Ref.	Debit	Credit	Balance
Aug.	1	Balance Forward	✓			6500 —

ACCOUNTS RECEIVABLE **ACCT. NO. 110**

Date		Explanation	Post. Ref.	Debit	Credit	Balance
Aug.	1	Balance Forward	✓			2100 —

NAME: ____________________

Problem 4.2 *(continued)*

Instructions 1 and 3

CLEANING SUPPLIES — ACCT. NO. 114

Date		Explanation	Post. Ref.	Debit	Credit	Balance
20XX Aug.	1	Balance Forward	✓			1950—

CLEANING EQUIPMENT — ACCT. NO. 115

Date		Explanation	Post. Ref.	Debit	Credit	Balance
20XX Aug.	1	Balance Forward	✓			95000—

OFFICE EQUIPMENT — ACCT. NO. 120

Date		Explanation	Post. Ref.	Debit	Credit	Balance
20XX Aug.	1	Balance Forward	✓			8000—

ACCOUNTS PAYABLE — ACCT. NO. 210

Date		Explanation	Post. Ref.	Debit	Credit	Balance
20XX Aug.	1	Balance Forward	✓			4500—

NOTES PAYABLE — ACCT. NO. 220

Date		Explanation	Post. Ref.	Debit	Credit	Balance
20XX Aug.	1	Balance Forward	✓			50000—

NATHANIEL EMERSON, CAPITAL — ACCT. NO. 310

Date		Explanation	Post. Ref.	Debit	Credit	Balance
20XX Aug.	1	Balance Forward	✓			59050—

NAME:________________________

Problem 4.2 *(continued)*

Instructions 1 and 3

NATHANIEL EMERSON, DRAWING — **ACCT. NO. 320**

Date	Explanation	Post. Ref.	Debit	Credit	Balance

CLEANING REVENUE — **ACCT. NO. 410**

Date	Explanation	Post. Ref.	Debit	Credit	Balance

RENT EXPENSE — **ACCT. NO. 601**

Date	Explanation	Post. Ref.	Debit	Credit	Balance

INSURANCE EXPENSE — **ACCT. NO. 605**

Date	Explanation	Post. Ref.	Debit	Credit	Balance

ADVERTISING EXPENSE — **ACCT. NO. 610**

Date	Explanation	Post. Ref.	Debit	Credit	Balance

SALARY EXPENSE — **ACCT. NO. 620**

Date	Explanation	Post. Ref.	Debit	Credit	Balance

UTILITIES EXPENSE — **ACCT. NO. 630**

Date	Explanation	Post. Ref.	Debit	Credit	Balance

NAME:________________________

Problem 4.2 *(continued)*

Instructions 1 and 3

INTEREST EXPENSE　　　　ACCT. NO. 635

Date		Explanation	Post. Ref.	Debit	Credit	Balance

Instruction 2

GENERAL JOURNAL　　　　PAGE NO.

Date		Description	Post. Ref.	Debit	Credit

NAME:______________________________

Problem 4.2 *(continued)*

Instruction 2

GENERAL JOURNAL PAGE NO.

Date		Description	Post. Ref.	Debit	Credit

NAME:____________________

Problem 4.2 *(continued)*

Instruction 2

GENERAL JOURNAL				PAGE NO.	
Date		Description	Post. Ref.	Debit	Credit

NAME:______________________________

Problem 4.2 *(continued)*

Instruction 4

____

____

____

NAME:______________________

Problem 4.2 *(continued)*

Instruction 5

____

____

____

Instruction 6

____

____

____

NAME:________________________

Problem 4.2 *(continued)*

Instruction 7

NAME:________________________

Problem 4.3

Instruction 1

GENERAL JOURNAL				PAGE NO. 1	
Date		Description	Post. Ref.	Debit	Credit
20XX Dec.	1	Cash		12000—	
		David Kowalczyk, Capital			12000—
		To record owner's investment			
	2	Equipment		4000—	
		Cash			1000—
		Accounts Receivable			3000—
		Bought equipment; paid $1,000 down;			
		balance due in 90 days			
	4	Furniture		2000—	
		Notes Payable			2000—
		Bought furniture; signed a 6-month, 7% note for $2,000			
	5	Cash		500—	
		Supplies			500—
		Paid cash for supplies			
	6	Cash		400—	
		Dance Revenue			400—
		To record week's revenue; $400 received in cash;			
		$300 balance due in 30 days			
	9	Utilities Expense		105—	
		Cash			105—
		Paid bill for electricity			

NAME:______________________

Problem 4.3 *(continued)*

Instruction 1 (continued)

GENERAL JOURNAL					PAGE NO.
Date		Description	Post. Ref.	Debit	Credit
20XX Dec.	10	Cash		370—	
		David Kowalczyk, Drawing			370—
		To record owner's withdrawal			
	12	Utilities Expense		75—	
		Accounts Payable			75—
		Received phone bill; record now to be paid later			
	15	Wages Expense		1200—	
		Cash			1200—
		To record wages of $800 and owner's withdrawal of $400			
	18	Utilities Expense		75—	
		Cash			75—
		Payment of phone bill received and recorded			
		Dec. 12			
	20	Cash		300—	
		David Kowalczyk, Capital			300—
		Cash received from charge customers			
	23	Advertising Expense		175—	
		Accounts Receivable			175—
		Bill received for newspaper ad in December			
	24	Equipment		1000—	
		David Kowalczyk, Capital			1000—
		Owner donated a computer to the business			

NAME:

Problem 4.3 *(continued)*

Instruction 1 (continued)

GENERAL JOURNAL — PAGE NO.

Date		Description	Post. Ref.	Debit	Credit
20XX Dec.	26	Wages Expense		700—	
		Cash			700—
		Wages of $700			
	28	Cash		500—	
		Accounts Payable		600	
		Dance Revenue			1100—
		Revenue of $1,100; $500 received in cash			
	30	Accounts Receivable		500—	
		Cash			500—
		Payment made on equipment purchased			
		on December 2			

NAME:____________________

Problem 4.3 *(continued)*

Instruction 2

GENERAL LEDGER

CASH **ACCT. NO. 110**

Date		Explanation	Post. Ref.	Debit	Credit	Balance

ACCOUNTS RECEIVABLE **ACCT. NO. 120**

Date		Explanation	Post. Ref.	Debit	Credit	Balance

SUPPLIES **ACCT. NO. 130**

Date		Explanation	Post. Ref.	Debit	Credit	Balance

NAME:

Problem 4.3 *(continued)*

Instruction 2

EQUIPMENT — ACCT. NO. 140

Date		Explanation	Post. Ref.	Debit	Credit	Balance

FURNITURE — ACCT. NO. 150

Date		Explanation	Post. Ref.	Debit	Credit	Balance

ACCOUNTS PAYABLE — ACCT. NO. 210

Date		Explanation	Post. Ref.	Debit	Credit	Balance

NOTES PAYABLE — ACCT. NO. 220

Date		Explanation	Post. Ref.	Debit	Credit	Balance

DAVID KOWALCZYK, CAPITAL — ACCT. NO. 310

Date		Explanation	Post. Ref.	Debit	Credit	Balance

DAVID KOWALCZYK, DRAWING — ACCT. NO. 320

Date		Explanation	Post. Ref.	Debit	Credit	Balance

NAME:________________________

Problem 4.3 *(continued)*

Instruction 2

DANCE REVENUE — **ACCT. NO. 410**

Date		Explanation	Post. Ref.	Debit	Credit	Balance

UTILITIES EXPENSE — **ACCT. NO. 610**

Date		Explanation	Post. Ref.	Debit	Credit	Balance

WAGES EXPENSE — **ACCT. NO. 620**

Date		Explanation	Post. Ref.	Debit	Credit	Balance

ADVERTISING EXPENSE — **ACCT. NO. 630**

Date		Explanation	Post. Ref.	Debit	Credit	Balance

NAME:________________________

Problem 4.3 *(continued)*

Instruction 3

Instruction 4

NAME:______________________________

Problem 4.3 *(continued)*

Instruction 5

NAME: ____________________

Problem 4.4

Instruction 1

GENERAL JOURNAL				PAGE NO.
Date	Description	Post. Ref.	Debit	Credit

NAME:______________________

Problem 4.4 *(continued)*

Instructions 2, 3 and 4

Error	Will revenue be over-stated? By how much?	Will revenue be under-stated? By how much?	Will expenses be over-stated? By how much?	Will expenses be under-stated? By how much?	Will net income be over-stated? By how much?	Will net income be under-stated By how much?
1.			yes, $700			yes, $700
2.						
3.						
4.						
5.						
6.						

Instruction 5

NAME:______________________

CHAPTER 5

Adjustments and the Ten-Column Worksheet

Vocabulary Review

1. ______________________
2. ______________________
3. ______________________
4. ______________________
5. ______________________
6. ______________________
7. ______________________
8. ______________________
9. ______________________
10. ______________________
11. ______________________
12. ______________________
13. ______________________
14. ______________________
15. ______________________
16. ______________________
17. ______________________
18. ______________________
19. ______________________
20. ______________________

NAME:________________________

Exercise 5.1

GENERAL JOURNAL					PAGE NO.
Date		Description	Post. Ref.	Debit	Credit

Exercise 5.2

GENERAL JOURNAL					PAGE NO.
Date		Description	Post. Ref.	Debit	Credit

NAME:____________________

Exercise 5.3

GENERAL JOURNAL					PAGE NO.
Date		Description	Post. Ref.	Debit	Credit

Exercise 5.4

GENERAL JOURNAL					PAGE NO.
Date		Description	Post. Ref.	Debit	Credit

NAME:______________________________

Exercise 5.5

GENERAL JOURNAL			PAGE NO.	
Date	Description	Post. Ref.	Debit	Credit

Exercise 5.6

GENERAL JOURNAL			PAGE NO.	
Date	Description	Post. Ref.	Debit	Credit

NAME: ____________________

Exercise 5.7

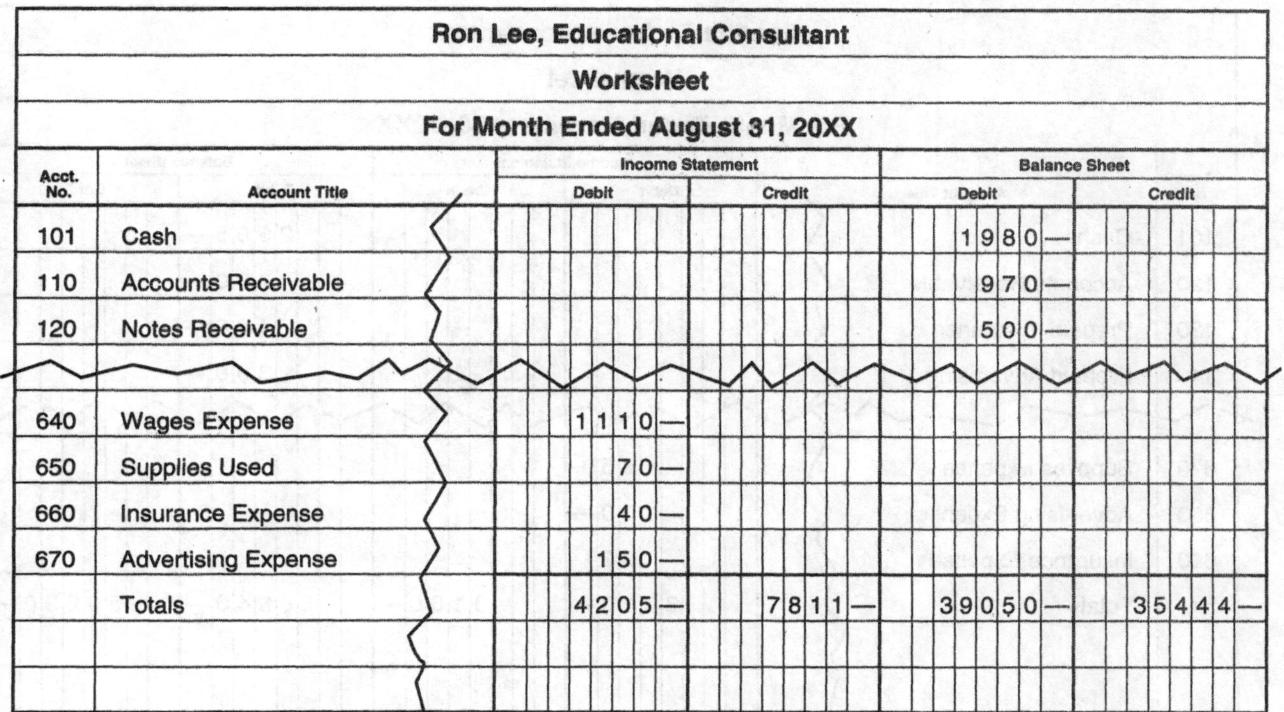

Ron Lee, Educational Consultant
Worksheet
For Month Ended August 31, 20XX

Acct. No.	Account Title	Income Statement Debit	Income Statement Credit	Balance Sheet Debit	Balance Sheet Credit
101	Cash			1980—	
110	Accounts Receivable			970—	
120	Notes Receivable			500—	
640	Wages Expense	1110—			
650	Supplies Used	70—			
660	Insurance Expense	40—			
670	Advertising Expense	150—			
	Totals	4205—	7811—	39050—	35444—

Exercise 5.8

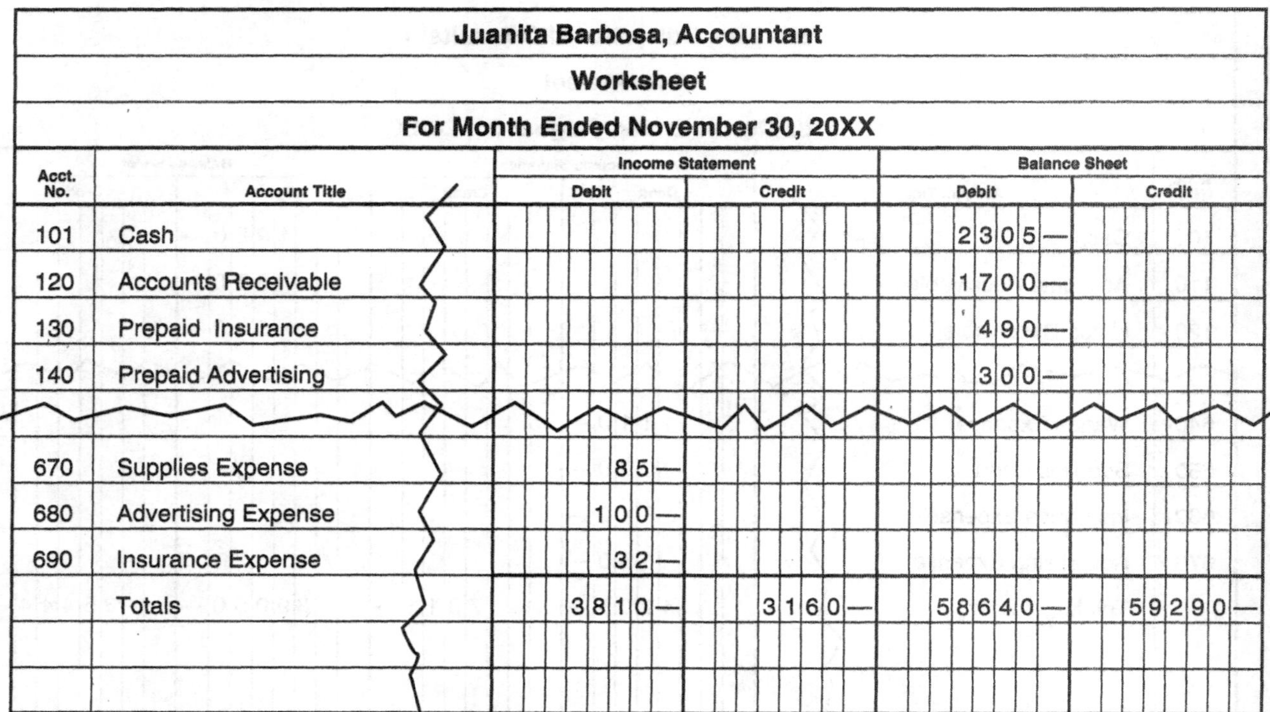

Juanita Barbosa, Accountant					
Worksheet					
For Month Ended November 30, 20XX					
		Income Statement		Balance Sheet	
Acct. No.	Account Title	Debit	Credit	Debit	Credit
101	Cash			2305—	
120	Accounts Receivable			1700—	
130	Prepaid Insurance			490—	
140	Prepaid Advertising			300—	
670	Supplies Expense	85—			
680	Advertising Expense	100—			
690	Insurance Expense	32—			
	Totals	3810—	3160—	58640—	59290—

NAME:________________________

Exercise 5.9

	Account Classification	Normal Debit or Credit Balance	Which Financial Statement
Example: Accounts Receivable	A	Debit	BS
a. Notes Payable			
b. Rent Expense			
c. Revenue from Consulting			
d. Office Equipment			
e. Supplies			
f. Supplies Expense			
g. Accumulated Amortization			
h. Prepaid Advertising			
i. Owner's Drawing			
j. Delivery Revenue			
k. Unearned Delivery Revenue			
l. Prepaid Rent			
m. Automobile			
n. Wages Payable			
o. Unearned Consulting Revenue			

NAME:______________________________

Exercise 5.10

George Atkinson, Consultant					
Worksheet					
For Month Ending September 30, 20XX					
		Unadjusted Trial Balance		Adjustments	
Acct. No.	Account Title	Debit	Credit	Debit	Credit
101	Cash	12000—			
105	Accounts Receivable	8500—		e) 1250—	
110	Notes Receivable	14000—			
115	Office Supplies	1500—			a) 400—
120	Prepaid Insurance	1290—			b) 100—
128	Office Equipment	22000—			
129	Accumulated Amortization: DE		5520—		d) 460—
201	Accounts Payable		1750—		
205	Notes Payable		9800—		
206	Payroll Taxes Payable		520—		
210	Unearned Revenue		1500—	f) 900—	
301	George Atkinson, Capital		42260—		
310	George Atkinson, Drawing	5000—			
401	Revenue from Teaching		8500—		e) 1250—
405	Revenue from Consulting		1500—		f) 900—
601	Rent Expense	2200—			
603	Utilities Expense	470—			
620	Advertising Expense	500—			
630	Wages Expense	3800—		c) 350—	
640	Interest Expense	90—			
	Totals	71350—	71350—		
650	Office Supplies Used			a) 400—	
615	Insurance Expense			b) 100—	
220	Wages Payable				c) 350—
660	Amortization Expense			d) 460—	
				3460—	3460—

NAME:________________________

Exercise 5.10 *(continued)*

Adjusted Trial Balance		Income Statement		Balance Sheet	
Debit	Credit	Debit	Credit	Debit	Credit

NAME:________________________

Exercise 5.11

	Over-statement of Expenses	Under-statement of Expenses	Over-statement of Revenue	Under-statement of Revenue	Over-statement of Net Income	Under-statement of Net Income
Example:		$1,000			$1,000	
a.						
b.						
c.						
d.						
e.						
f.						
g.						

Problem 5.1

Instructions 1, 2, 3, 4, 5, 6 and 7

NAME: ____________________

Linowitz Trucking Company					
Worksheet					
For Month Ended May 31, 19XX					
Acct. No.	**Account Title**	**Unadjusted Trial Balance**		**Adjustments**	
		Debit	**Credit**	**Debit**	**Credit**
110	Cash	28000—			
115	Accounts Receivable	4320—		g) 4900—	
120	Notes Receivable	7600—			
125	Office Supplies	1490—			a) 560—
130	Trucking Supplies	7130—			b) 1840—
140	Prepaid Insurance	4700—			c) 300—
150	Prepaid Advertising	6900—			d) 2300—
160	Equipment	142000—			
161	Acc. Amortization – Equip.		37760—		e) 2360—
170	Trucks	732000—			
171	Acc. Amortization – Trucks		195200—		e) 12200—
180	Office Furniture	3970—			
181	Acc. Amortization – Office Furniture		1120—		e) 70—
200	Accounts Payable		6900—		
210	Notes Payable		416500—		
220	Payroll Taxes Payable		800—		
230	Unearned Revenue		4250—	h) 2000—	
300	P. Linowitz, Capital		264101—		
310	P. Linowitz, Drawing	3250—			
400	Trucking Revenue		37650—		g) 4900—
					h) 2000—
610	Interest Expense	6247—			
620	Rent Expense	1800—			
630	Repairs Expense	2404—			
640	Gas & Oil Expense	3170—			
650	Utilities Expense	1200—			
660	Wages Expense	8100—		f) 950—	
	Totals	964281—	964281—		
605	Office Supplies Expense			a) 560—	
615	Truck Supplies Expense			b) 1840—	
625	Insurance Expense			c) 300—	
635	Advertising Expense			d) 2300—	
645	Amortization Expense			e) 14630—	
240	Wages Payable				f) 950—
				27480—	27480—

Problem 5.1 *(continued)*

NAME:__________________________

Instructions 1, 2, 3, 4, 5, 6 and 7

Adjusted Trial Balance		Income Statement		Balance Sheet	
Debit	Credit	Debit	Credit	Debit	Credit

NAME:______________________________

Problem 5.1

Instruction 8

GENERAL JOURNAL				PAGE NO.
Date	Description	Post. Ref.	Debit	Credit

NAME:______________________

Problem 5.2

Instructions 1, 2 and 3

Carol's Exercise Clinic Worksheet For Month Ended June 30, 20XX					
		Unadjusted Trial Balance		Adjustments	
Acct. No.	Account Title	Debit	Credit	Debit	Credit
101	Cash	4250—			
105	Accounts Receivable	1535—			
110	Notes Receivable	1690—			
120	Supplies	615—			
130	Prepaid Insurance	500—			
140	Van	23600—			
141	Acc. Amortization – Van		10200—		
150	Equipment	48000—			
151	Acc. Amortization – Equipment		2000—		
201	Accounts Payable		400—		
205	Notes Payable		10000—		
210	Unearned Revenue		1000—		
220	Mortgage Payable		43000—		
305	Carol Goren, Capital		14590—		
310	Carol Goren, Drawing	2600—			
401	Revenue – Teaching		750—		
410	Revenue – Ex. Clinic		6200—		
602	Utilities Expense	195—			
604	Advertising Expense	250—			
610	Interest Expense	760—			
620	Wages Expense	2800—			
630	Payroll Taxes Expense	170—			
635	Gas & Oil Expense	130—			
650	Repairs Expense	225—			
660	Insurance Expense	820—			
	Totals	88140—	88140—		
670	Supplies Expense				
685	Amortization Expense				
230	Wages Payable				

NAME:________________________

Problem 5.2 *(continued)*

Instructions 1, 2 and 3

Adjusted Trial Balance		Income Statement		Balance Sheet	
Debit	Credit	Debit	Credit	Debit	Credit

NAME:______________________________

Problem 5.2 *(continued)*

Instruction 4

GENERAL JOURNAL				PAGE NO.	
Date		Description	Post. Ref.	Debit	Credit

NAME:______________________

Problem 5.3

Instructions 1, 2 and 3

Dancing Dynamics					
Worksheet					
For the Three-Month Period Ending March 31, 20XX					
		Unadjusted Trial Balance		Adjustments	
Acct. No.	Account Title	Debit	Credit	Debit	Credit
101	Cash	1950 —			
105	Accounts Receivable	2700 —			
110	Supplies	560 —			
115	Prepaid Insurance	400 —			
120	Office Equipment	11500 —			
121	Acc. Amortization – Office Equip.				
145	Van	18000 —			
146	Acc. Amortization – Van				
201	Accounts Payable		3520 —		
210	Notes Payable		15500 —		
215	Payroll Taxes Payable		145 —		
220	Interest Payable		335 —		
230	Unearned Lecturing Revenue		1500 —		
301	Jon Phillips, Capital		16370 —		
310	Jon Phillips, Drawing	4000 —			
401	Revenue from Dancing		10520 —		
410	Revenue from Lecturing		840 —		
601	Rent Expense	2400 —			
610	Utilities Expense	600 —			
615	Advertising Expense	450 —			
620	Repairs Expense	420 —			
630	Gas & Oil Expense	550 —			
640	Interest Expense	1000 —			
650	Wages Expense	4200 —			
	Totals	48730 —	48730 —		
660	Supplies Expense				
670	Insurance Expense				
680	Amortization Expense				
240	Wages Payable				

NAME:____________________

Problem 5.3 *(continued)*

Instructions 1, 2 and 3

Adjusted Trial Balance		Income Statement		Balance Sheet	
Debit	Credit	Debit	Credit	Debit	Credit

NAME:______________________________

Problem 5.3 *(continued)*

Instruction 4

____

____

____

NAME: ____________________

Problem 5.3 *(continued)*

Instruction 5

GENERAL JOURNAL				PAGE NO.	
Date		Description	Post. Ref.	Debit	Credit

NAME:____________________

Problem 5.4

Instructions 1, 2 and 3

Marie's Bookkeeping Service						
Worksheet						
For the Third Quarter of 20XX						
Acct. No.	Account Title	Unadjusted Trial Balance		Adjustments		
		Debit	Credit	Debit	Credit	
101	Cash	4120 —				
110	Accounts Receivable	1780 —				
115	Office Supplies	920 —				
120	Prepaid Insurance	300 —				
125	Prepaid Advertising	600 —				
130	Office Equipment	18050 —				
131	Acc. Amortization – Office Equip.		3000 —			
150	Automobile	14800 —				
151	Acc.Amortization – Automobile		4500 —			
201	Accounts Payable		1100 —			
210	Notes Payable		12000 —			
215	Payroll Taxes Pay		144 —			
230	Unearned Consulting Revenue		900 —			
301	Marie Himler, Capital		15066 —			
310	Marie Himler, Drawing	3600 —				
401	Revenue from Bookkeeping		8950 —			
410	Revenue from Consulting		4750 —			
601	Rent Expense	1800 —				
610	Repairs Expense	475 —				
620	Utilities Expense	450 —				
630	Advertising Expense	600 —				
640	Insurance Expense	305 —				
650	Gas & Oil Expense	210 —				
660	Wages Expense	2400 —				
	Totals	50410 —	50410 —			
670	Supplies Expense					
680	Amortization Expense					
250	Wages Payable					

NAME:______________________

Problem 5.4 *(continued)*

Instructions 1, 2 and 3

Adjusted Trial Balance		Income Statement		Balance Sheet	
Debit	Credit	Debit	Credit	Debit	Credit

NAME:______________________________

Problem 5.4 *(continued)*

Instruction 4

____

____

____

NAME: ______________________

Problem 5.4 *(continued)*

Instruction 5

NAME:________________________

Problem 5.4 *(continued)*

Instruction 6

____

____

____

NAME:________________________

Problem 5.4 *(continued)*

Instruction 7

GENERAL JOURNAL				PAGE NO.
Date	Description	Post. Ref.	Debit	Credit

NAME:______________________

Problem 5.5

Instructions 1, 2, 3 and 4

Lori's Landscape Service
Worksheet
For Month Ending April 30, 20XX

Acct. No.	Account Title	Unadjusted Trial Balance Debit	Unadjusted Trial Balance Credit	Adjustments Debit	Adjustments Credit
101	Cash	3050—			
105	Accounts Receivable	1605—		g) 500—	
115	Office Supplies	495—			b) 205—
120	Garden Supplies	1840—			a) 720—
130	Prepaid Insurance	900—			c) 100—
140	Prepaid Advertising	800—			d) 200—
150	Office Equipment	8500—			
151	Acc. Amortization – Office Equip.		2300—		e) 150—
160	Garden Equipment	10000—			
161	Acc. Amortization – Garden Equip.		4900—		e) 230—
170	Truck	25500—			
171	Acc. Amortization – Truck		10600—		e) 400—
201	Accounts Payable		1400—		
210	Notes Payable		15200—		
215	Payroll Taxes Payable		160—		
220	Unearned Landscape Revenue		1000—	h) 600—	
301	Lori Salzman, Capital		17970—		
310	Lori Salzman, Drawing	2000—			
401	Landscape Revenue		4750—		g) 500—
					h) 600—
601	Truck Expense	760—			
610	Repairs Expense	290—			
620	Rent Expense	550—			
630	Wages Expense	1600—		f) 340—	
640	Utilities Expense	390—			
	Totals	58280—	58280—		
650	Garden Supplies Expense			a) 720—	
660	Office Supplies Expense			b) 205—	
670	Insurance Expense			c) 100—	
680	Advertising Expense			d) 200—	
690	Amortization Expense			e) 780—	
230	Wages Payable				f) 340—
				3445—	3445—

NAME:______________________________

Problem 5.5 *(continued)*

Instructions 1, 2, 3 and 4 (continued)

Adjusted Trial Balance		Income Statement		Balance Sheet	
Debit	Credit	Debit	Credit	Debit	Credit
3050—				3050—	
1105—				1105—	
290—				290—	
1130—				1310—	
800—				800—	
1000—				1000—	
8500—				8500—	
	2450—				2450—
10000—				10000—	
	5220—				5220—
25500—				25500—	
	1100—				1100—
	1400—				1400—
	15200—				15200—
	160—				160—
	1600—				1600—
	19790—				19970—
2000—					
	4750—		4750—		
670—		670—			
290—		290—			
550—		550—			
1600—		1600—			
390—		390—			
720—		720—			
250—		250—			
100—		100—			
200—		200—			
780—		780—			
	340—	340—			

NAME:______________________

Problem 5.6

Instruction 1

	Reduces Net Income by this amount	Increases Net Income by this amount
a.	$3,500	
b.		
c.		
d.		
e.		
f.		

Instruction 2

Net Income before adjustments	$5,700
Reduced by	
Subtotal	
Increased by	
Corrected Net Income	

NAME:______________________

Correcting and Closing Entries

Vocabulary Review

1. ______________________
2. ______________________
3. ______________________
4. ______________________
5. ______________________
6. ______________________
7. ______________________
8. ______________________
9. ______________________
10. ______________________
11. ______________________
12. ______________________
13. ______________________
14. ______________________
15. ______________________
16. ______________________
17. ______________________
18. ______________________

NAME:__________________________

Exercise 6.1

GENERAL JOURNAL					PAGE NO.
Date		Description	Post. Ref.	Debit	Credit

NAME:____________________________

Exercise 6.2

GENERAL LEDGER

DANIEL BLACK, CAPITAL — **ACCT. NO. 301**

Date		Explanation	Post. Ref.	Debit	Credit	Balance
20XX July	31	Balance	✓			8750—

DANIEL BLACK, DRAWING — **ACCT. NO. 310**

Date		Explanation	Post. Ref.	Debit	Credit	Balance
20XX July	31	Balance	✓			2400—

INCOME SUMMARY — **ACCT. NO. 315**

Date		Explanation	Post. Ref.	Debit	Credit	Balance

REVENUE — **ACCT. NO. 401**

Date		Explanation	Post. Ref.	Debit	Credit	Balance
20XX July	31	Balance	✓			4000—

UTILITIES EXPENSE — **ACCT. NO. 601**

Date		Explanation	Post. Ref.	Debit	Credit	Balance
20XX July	31	Balance	✓			190—

NAME:________________________

Exercise 6.2 *(continued)*

RENT EXPENSE **ACCT. NO. 605**

Date		Explanation	Post. Ref.	Debit	Credit	Balance
20XX July	31	Balance	✓			575 —

WAGES EXPENSE **ACCT. NO. 610**

Date		Explanation	Post. Ref.	Debit	Credit	Balance
20XX July	31	Balance	✓			900 —

ADVERTISING EXPENSE **ACCT. NO. 615**

Date		Explanation	Post. Ref.	Debit	Credit	Balance
20XX July	31	Balance	✓			250 —

PAYROLL TAX EXPENSE **ACCT. NO. 620**

Date		Explanation	Post. Ref.	Debit	Credit	Balance
20XX July	31	Balance	✓			55 —

SUPPLIES EXPENSE **ACCT. NO. 630**

Date		Explanation	Post. Ref.	Debit	Credit	Balance
20XX July	31	Balance	✓			70 —

AMORTIZATION EXPENSE **ACCT. NO. 640**

Date		Explanation	Post. Ref.	Debit	Credit	Balance
20XX July	31	Balance	✓			50 —

NAME:____________________

Exercise 6.3

GENERAL JOURNAL **PAGE NO.**

Date	Description	Post. Ref.	Debit	Credit

NAME: ____________________

Exercise 6.3 *(continued)*

Wayne Werner, Capital	301
	6/1 Balance 5,250

Wayne Werner, Drawing	310
6/30 Balance 1,000	

Income Summary	315

Revenue	401
	6/30 Balance 2,100

Rent Expense	601
6/30 Balance 400	

Insurance Expense	605
6/30 Balance 75	

Advertising Expense	610
6/30 Balance 250	

Repairs Expense	615
6/30 Balance 320	

Amortization Expense	650
6/30 Balance 450	

Supplies Expense	660
6/30 Balance 30	

Exercise 6.4

a. ____________________

b. ____________________

c. ____________________

d. ____________________

e. ____________________

f. ____________________

g. ____________________

h. ____________________

i. ____________________

j. ____________________

NAME: ______________________

Exercise 6.5

	Which Financial Statement?	Normal Debit or Credit Balance?
Example: Capital	Balance Sheet	Credit
a. Equipment		
b. Wages Payable		
c. Supplies Expense		
d. Accumulated Amortization		
e. Unearned Consulting Revenue		
f. Prepaid Advertising		
g. Wages Expense		
h. Supplies		
i. Revenue from Services		
j. Advertising Expense		
k. Prepaid Insurance		
l. Amortization Expense		
m. Unearned Medical Revenue		
n. Insurance Expense		
o. Consulting Revenue		

NAME:________________________

Exercise 6.6

GENERAL JOURNAL				PAGE NO.	
Date		Description	Post. Ref.	Debit	Credit

NAME: ______________________

Exercise 6.7

____

____

____

Exercise 6.8

1. ______________________________
2. ______________________________
3. ______________________________
4. ______________________________
5. ______________________________

   ____
6. ______________________________

   ____

NAME:________________

Exercise 6.9

GENERAL JOURNAL				PAGE NO. 4	
Date		Description	Post. Ref.	Debit	Credit
May	31	Income Summary		318—	
		Gregory Bronski, Capital			318—
		To transfer net income to capital			
	31	Gregory Bronski, Drawing		1800—	
		Gregory Bronski, Capital			1800—
		To transfer balance of drawing to capital			

Exercise 6.10

	Will error affect Net Income?	If so, will it be overstated, or understated?	By how much?
a.			
b.			
c.			
d.			
e.			
f.			
g.			
h.			
i.			
j.			

NAME:______________________

Problem 6.1

GENERAL JOURNAL				PAGE NO.	
Date		Description	Post. Ref.	Debit	Credit

NAME:________________________

Problem 6.1 *(continued)*

GENERAL JOURNAL			PAGE NO.		
Date		Description	Post. Ref.	Debit	Credit

NAME:____________________

Problem 6.2

Instruction 1

GENERAL JOURNAL PAGE NO.

Date		Description	Post. Ref.	Debit	Credit

NAME:______________________________

Problem 6.2 *(continued)*

Instruction 2

GENERAL LEDGER

CASH **ACCT. NO. 101**

Date		Explanation	Post. Ref.	Debit	Credit	Balance
20XX Sept.	30	Balance	✓			4020—

ACCOUNTS RECEIVABLE **ACCT. NO. 105**

Date		Explanation	Post. Ref.	Debit	Credit	Balance
20XX Sept.	30	Balance	✓			850—

SUPPLIES **ACCT. NO. 110**

Date		Explanation	Post. Ref.	Debit	Credit	Balance
20XX Sept.	30	Balance	✓			490—

PREPAID INSURANCE **ACCT. NO. 115**

Date		Explanation	Post. Ref.	Debit	Credit	Balance
20XX Sept.	30	Balance	✓			300—

EQUIPMENT **ACCT. NO. 120**

Date		Explanation	Post. Ref.	Debit	Credit	Balance
20XX Sept.	30	Balance	✓			3465—

ACCUMULATED AMORTIZATION: EQUIPMENT **ACCT. NO. 121**

Date		Explanation	Post. Ref.	Debit	Credit	Balance
20XX Sept.	30	Balance	✓			1590—

NAME:______________________

Problem 6.2 *(continued)*

Instruction 2

TRUCK — **ACCT. NO. 130**

Date		Explanation	Post. Ref.	Debit	Credit	Balance
20XX Sept.	30	Balance	✓			18500—

ACCUMULATED AMORTIZATION: TRUCK — **ACCT. NO. 131**

Date		Explanation	Post. Ref.	Debit	Credit	Balance
20XX Sept.	30	Balance	✓			8200—

ACCOUNTS PAYABLE — **ACCT. NO. 201**

Date		Explanation	Post. Ref.	Debit	Credit	Balance
20XX Sept.	30	Balance	✓			300—

NOTES PAYABLE — **ACCT. NO. 210**

Date		Explanation	Post. Ref.	Debit	Credit	Balance
20XX Sept.	30	Balance	✓			10550—

UNEARNED DELIVERY REVENUE — **ACCT. NO. 220**

Date		Explanation	Post. Ref.	Debit	Credit	Balance
20XX Sept.	30	Balance	✓			800—

DEE SNYDER, CAPITAL — **ACCT. NO. 301**

Date		Explanation	Post. Ref.	Debit	Credit	Balance
20XX Sept.	30	Balance	✓			7870—

DEE SNYDER, DRAWING — **ACCT. NO. 310**

Date		Explanation	Post. Ref.	Debit	Credit	Balance
20XX Sept.	30	Balance	✓			3200—

NAME:________________________

Problem 6.2 *(continued)*

Instruction 2

INCOME SUMMARY **ACCT. NO. 315**

Date		Explanation	Post. Ref.	Debit	Credit	Balance

REVENUE FROM DELIVERY **ACCT. NO. 401**

Date		Explanation	Post. Ref.	Debit	Credit	Balance
20XX Sept.	30	Balance	✓			4720—

TRUCK EXPENSE **ACCT. NO. 601**

Date		Explanation	Post. Ref.	Debit	Credit	Balance
20XX Sept.	30	Balance	✓			310—

RENT EXPENSE **ACCT. NO. 610**

Date		Explanation	Post. Ref.	Debit	Credit	Balance
20XX Sept.	30	Balance	✓			950—

UTILITIES EXPENSE **ACCT. NO. 615**

Date		Explanation	Post. Ref.	Debit	Credit	Balance
20XX Sept.	30	Balance	✓			255—

ADVERTISING EXPENSE **ACCT. NO. 630**

Date		Explanation	Post. Ref.	Debit	Credit	Balance
20XX Sept.	30	Balance	✓			580—

NAME:________________________

Problem 6.2 *(continued)*

Instruction 2

INTEREST EXPENSE — **ACCT. NO. 640**

Date		Explanation	Post. Ref.	Debit	Credit	Balance
20XX Sept.	30	Balance	✓			260 —

INSURANCE EXPENSE — **ACCT. NO. 650**

Date		Explanation	Post. Ref.	Debit	Credit	Balance
20XX Sept.	30	Balance	✓			100 —

SUPPLIES EXPENSE — **ACCT. NO. 660**

Date		Explanation	Post. Ref.	Debit	Credit	Balance
20XX Sept.	30	Balance	✓			75 —

AMORTIZATION EXPENSE — **ACCT. NO. 670**

Date		Explanation	Post. Ref.	Debit	Credit	Balance
20XX Sept.	30	Balance	✓			675 —

NAME:________________________

Problem 6.2 *(continued)*

Instruction 3

NAME:____________________

Problem 6.3

Instruction 1

GENERAL JOURNAL			PAGE NO.	
Date	Description	Post. Ref.	Debit	Credit

NAME: ______________________

Problem 6.3 *(continued)*

Instruction 2

____

____

____

Instruction 3

____

____

____

NAME:________________________

Problem 6.3 *(continued)*

Instruction 4

NAME:______________________________

Problem 6.4

Instruction 1

GENERAL JOURNAL				PAGE NO.	
Date		Description	Post. Ref.	Debit	Credit

NAME: ____________________

Problem 6.4 *(continued)*

Instruction 2

GENERAL JOURNAL			PAGE NO.	
Date	Description	Post. Ref.	Debit	Credit

NAME:______________________

Problem 6.4 *(continued)*

Instructions 1 and 2

GENERAL LEDGER

CASH **ACCT. NO. 101**

Date		Explanation	Post. Ref.	Debit	Credit	Balance
20XX Dec.	31	Balance	✓			6400—

ACCOUNTS RECEIVABLE **ACCT. NO. 110**

Date		Explanation	Post. Ref.	Debit	Credit	Balance
20XX Dec.	31	Balance	✓			1250—

BEAUTY SUPPLIES **ACCT. NO. 120**

Date		Explanation	Post. Ref.	Debit	Credit	Balance
20XX Dec.	31	Balance	✓			2800—

OFFICE SUPPLIES **ACCT. NO. 125**

Date		Explanation	Post. Ref.	Debit	Credit	Balance
20XX Dec.	31	Balance	✓			980—

PREPAID INSURANCE **ACCT. NO. 130**

Date		Explanation	Post. Ref.	Debit	Credit	Balance
20XX Dec.	31	Balance	✓			1440—

HAIR STYLING EQUIPMENT **ACCT. NO. 135**

Date		Explanation	Post. Ref.	Debit	Credit	Balance
20XX Dec.	31	Balance	✓			18000—

NAME:____________________

Problem 6.4 *(continued)*

Instructions 1 and 2

ACC. AMORTIZATION: HAIR STYLING EQUIPMENT — ACCT. NO. 136

Date		Explanation	Post. Ref.	Debit	Credit	Balance
20XX Dec.	31	Balance	✓			550 0—

OFFICE EQUIPMENT — ACCT. NO. 140

Date		Explanation	Post. Ref.	Debit	Credit	Balance
20XX Dec.	31	Balance	✓			1050 0—

ACC. AMORTIZATION: OFFICE EQUIPMENT — ACCT. NO. 141

Date		Explanation	Post. Ref.	Debit	Credit	Balance
20XX Dec.	31	Balance	✓			1837—

FURNITURE — ACCT. NO. 150

Date		Explanation	Post. Ref.	Debit	Credit	Balance
20XX Dec.	31	Balance	✓			6200—

ACC. AMORTIZATION: FURNITURE — ACCT. NO. 151

Date		Explanation	Post. Ref.	Debit	Credit	Balance
20XX Dec.	31	Balance	✓			1100—

AUTOMOBILE — ACCT. NO. 160

Date		Explanation	Post. Ref.	Debit	Credit	Balance
20XX Dec.	31	Balance	✓			18200—

NAME:_______________

Problem 6.4 *(continued)*

Instructions 1 and 2

ACCUMULATED AMORTIZATION: AUTOMOBILE **ACCT. NO. 161**

Date		Explanation	Post. Ref.	Debit	Credit	Balance
20XX Dec.	31	Balance	✓			3663—

ACCOUNTS PAYABLE **ACCT. NO. 205**

Date		Explanation	Post. Ref.	Debit	Credit	Balance
20XX Dec.	31	Balance	✓			2940—

NOTES PAYABLE **ACCT. NO. 220**

Date		Explanation	Post. Ref.	Debit	Credit	Balance
20XX Dec.	31	Balance	✓			15600—

UNEARNED HAIR STYLING REVENUE **ACCT. NO. 230**

Date		Explanation	Post. Ref.	Debit	Credit	Balance
20XX Dec.	31	Balance	✓			500—

WAGES PAYABLE **ACCT. NO. 240**

Date		Explanation	Post. Ref.	Debit	Credit	Balance

ROBERT GOODWIN, CAPITAL **ACCT. NO. 301**

Date		Explanation	Post. Ref.	Debit	Credit	Balance
20XX Dec.	31	Balance	✓			36526—

NAME: ______________________

Problem 6.4 *(continued)*

Instructions 1 and 2

ROBERT GOODWIN, DRAWING — **ACCT. NO. 310**

Date		Explanation	Post. Ref.	Debit	Credit	Balance
20XX Dec.	31	Balance	✓			2500—

INCOME SUMMARY — **ACCT. NO. 315**

Date		Explanation	Post. Ref.	Debit	Credit	Balance

HAIR STYLING REVENUE — **ACCT. NO. 401**

Date		Explanation	Post. Ref.	Debit	Credit	Balance
20XX Dec.	31	Balance	✓			6150—

RENT EXPENSE — **ACCT. NO. 601**

Date		Explanation	Post. Ref.	Debit	Credit	Balance
20XX Dec.	31	Balance	✓			1800—

ADVERTISING EXPENSE — **ACCT. NO. 610**

Date		Explanation	Post. Ref.	Debit	Credit	Balance
20XX Dec.	31	Balance	✓			500—

BEAUTY SUPPLIES EXPENSE — **ACCT. NO. 615**

Date		Explanation	Post. Ref.	Debit	Credit	Balance

NAME:______________________

Problem 6.4 *(continued)*

Instructions 1 and 2

UTILITIES EXPENSE — ACCT. NO. 620

Date		Explanation	Post. Ref.	Debit	Credit	Balance
20XX Dec.	31	Balance	✓			470 —

OFFICE SUPPLIES EXPENSE — ACCT. NO. 625

Date		Explanation	Post. Ref.	Debit	Credit	Balance

REPAIRS EXPENSE — ACCT. NO. 630

Date		Explanation	Post. Ref.	Debit	Credit	Balance
20XX Dec.	31	Balance	✓			220 —

INSURANCE EXPENSE — ACCT. NO. 635

Date		Explanation	Post. Ref.	Debit	Credit	Balance

INTEREST EXPENSE — ACCT. NO. 640

Date		Explanation	Post. Ref.	Debit	Credit	Balance
20XX Dec.	31	Balance	✓			156 —

WAGES EXPENSE — ACCT. NO. 650

Date		Explanation	Post. Ref.	Debit	Credit	Balance
20XX Dec.	31	Balance	✓			2200 —

NAME:____________________

Problem 6.4 *(continued)*

Instructions 1 and 2

PAYROLL TAX EXPENSE **ACCT. NO. 655**

Date		Explanation	Post. Ref.	Debit	Credit	Balance
20XX Dec.	31	Balance	✓			200—

AMORTIZATION EXPENSE **ACCT. NO. 670**

Date		Explanation	Post. Ref.	Debit	Credit	Balance

NAME:____________________

Problem 6.4 *(continued)*

Instruction 3

____

____

____

NAME:

Problem 6.4 *(continued)*

Instruction 4

NAME:________________________

Problem 6.4 *(continued)*

Instruction 4

NAME:______________________________

Problem 6.4 *(continued)*

Instruction 5

____

____

____

NAME:______________________

Problem 6.5

Instructions 1, 2 and 3

Uncle Ray's Party Service Worksheet For the Third Quarter Ended September 30, 20XX					
Acct. No.	Account Title	Unadjusted Trial Balance		Adjustments	
		Debit	Credit	Debit	Credit
101	Cash	5214 —			
110	Accounts Receivable	279 —			
115	Party Supplies	895 —			
116	Prepaid Insurance	300 —			
120	Party Equipment	6500 —			
121	Acc. Amortization – Party Equip.		750 —		
130	Van	18000 —			
131	Acc. Amortization – Van		1250 —		
201	Accounts Payable		756 —		
205	Notes Payable		11404 —		
210	Unearned Party Revenue		600 —		
301	R. Whittier, Capital		19714 —		
310	R. Whittier, Drawing	4500 —			
401	Revenue from Party Services		8742 —		
601	Wages Expense	4046 —			
610	Repairs Expense	750 —			
620	Rent Expense	1500 —			
630	Payroll Tax Expense	125 —			
640	Utilities Expense	507 —			
670	Advertising Expense	600 —			
	Totals	43216 —	43216 —		
680	Party Supplies Expense				
690	Insurance Expense				
675	Amortization Expense				
220	Wages Payable				

NAME:______________________________

Problem 6.5 *(continued)*

Instructions 1, 2 and 3

Adjusted Trial Balance		Income Statement		Balance Sheet	
Debit	Credit	Debit	Credit	Debit	Credit

NAME:____________________

Problem 6.5 *(continued)*

Instructions 4 and 5

GENERAL JOURNAL				PAGE NO.	
Date		Description	Post. Ref.	Debit	Credit

NAME:________________________

Problem 6.5 *(continued)*

Instructions 4 and 5

GENERAL JOURNAL				PAGE NO.	
Date		Description	Post. Ref.	Debit	Credit

NAME: ____________________

Problem 6.6

Instruction 1

a.

Accounts Receivable	**110**
Balance	
Correction	
Balance	

Accounts Payable	**210**
	Balance
Correction	
	Balance

b.

c.

d.

e.

f.

g.

NAME:____________________

Problem 6.6 *(continued)*

Instruction 2

____

____

____

NAME:________________________

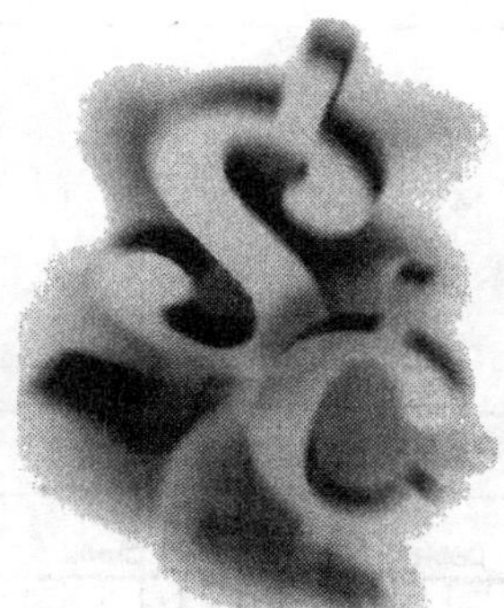

Comprehensive Problem 1

Instructions 2, 10 and 12

GENERAL JOURNAL				PAGE NO.	
Date		Description	Post. Ref.	Debit	Credit

NAME:

Comprehensive Problem 1 *(continued)*

Instructions 2, 10 and 12

GENERAL JOURNAL — **PAGE NO.**

Date		Description	Post. Ref.	Debit	Credit

NAME:______________________

Comprehensive Problem 1 *(continued)*

Instructions 2, 10 and 12

GENERAL JOURNAL			PAGE NO.	
Date	Description	Post. Ref.	Debit	Credit

NAME:____________________

Comprehensive Problem 1 *(continued)*

Instructions 2, 10 and 12

GENERAL JOURNAL PAGE NO.

Date	Description	Post. Ref.	Debit	Credit

NAME: ____________________

Comprehensive Problem 1 *(continued)*

Instructions 2, 10 and 12

GENERAL JOURNAL			PAGE NO.	
Date	Description	Post. Ref.	Debit	Credit

NAME:______________________________

Comprehensive Problem 1 *(continued)*

Instructions 2, 10 and 12

GENERAL JOURNAL				PAGE NO.
Date	Description	Post. Ref.	Debit	Credit

NAME:______________________

Comprehensive Problem 1 *(continued)*

Instructions 2, 10 and 12

GENERAL JOURNAL				PAGE NO.
Date	Description	Post. Ref.	Debit	Credit

NAME:____________________________

Comprehensive Problem 1 *(continued)*

Instructions 1, 3, 11 and 13

GENERAL LEDGER

CASH **ACCT. NO. 110**

Date		Explanation	Post. Ref.	Debit	Credit	Balance
20XX Oct.	1	Balance	✓			1754063

NAME:________________________

Comprehensive Problem 1 *(continued)*

Instructions 1, 3, 11 and 13

ACCOUNTS RECEIVABLE **ACCT. NO. 120**

Date		Explanation	Post. Ref.	Debit	Credit	Balance
20XX Oct.	1	Balance	✓			12409 15

SUPPLIES **ACCT. NO. 130**

Date		Explanation	Post. Ref.	Debit	Credit	Balance
20XX Oct.	1	Balance	✓			1962 —

PREPAID INSURANCE **ACCT. NO. 135**

Date		Explanation	Post. Ref.	Debit	Credit	Balance
20XX Oct.	1	Balance	✓			600 —

LAND **ACCT. NO. 138**

Date		Explanation	Post. Ref.	Debit	Credit	Balance
20XX Oct.	1	Balance	✓			36000 —

EQUIPMENT **ACCT. NO. 140**

Date		Explanation	Post. Ref.	Debit	Credit	Balance
20XX Oct.	1	Balance	✓			75000 —

NAME:________________________

Comprehensive Problem 1 *(continued)*

Instructions 1, 3, 11 and 13

ACCUMULATED AMORTIZATION: EQUIPMENT — **ACCT. NO. 141**

Date		Explanation	Post. Ref.	Debit	Credit	Balance
20XX Oct.	1	Balance	✓			19800—

DELIVERY VAN — **ACCT. NO. 150**

Date		Explanation	Post. Ref.	Debit	Credit	Balance
20XX Oct.	1	Balance	✓			21640—

ACCUMULATED AMORTIZATION: DELIVERY VAN — **ACCT. NO. 151**

Date		Explanation	Post. Ref.	Debit	Credit	Balance
20XX Oct.	1	Balance	✓			10800—

FURNITURE — **ACCT. NO. 160**

Date		Explanation	Post. Ref.	Debit	Credit	Balance
20XX Oct.	1	Balance	✓			4300—

ACCUMULATED AMORTIZATION: FURNITURE — **ACCT. NO. 161**

Date		Explanation	Post. Ref.	Debit	Credit	Balance
20XX Oct.	1	Balance	✓			2145—

BUILDING — **ACCT. NO. 170**

Date		Explanation	Post. Ref.	Debit	Credit	Balance
20XX Oct.	1	Balance	✓			195000—

ACCUMULATED AMORTIZATION: BUILDING — **ACCT. NO. 171**

Date		Explanation	Post. Ref.	Debit	Credit	Balance
20XX Oct.	1	Balance	✓			24750—

NAME:______________________

Comprehensive Problem 1 *(continued)*

Instructions 1, 3, 11 and 13

ACCOUNTS PAYABLE — **ACCT. NO. 210**

Date		Explanation	Post. Ref.	Debit	Credit	Balance
20XX Oct.	1	Balance	✓			4203 32

NOTES PAYABLE — **ACCT. NO. 220**

Date		Explanation	Post. Ref.	Debit	Credit	Balance
20XX Oct.	1	Balance	✓			31490 60

UNEARNED CONSULTING REVENUE — **ACCT. NO. 225**

Date		Explanation	Post. Ref.	Debit	Credit	Balance

MORTGAGE PAYABLE: BUILDING — **ACCT. NO. 230**

Date		Explanation	Post. Ref.	Debit	Credit	Balance
20XX Oct.	1	Balance	✓			122400 —

WAGES PAYABLE — **ACCT. NO. 240**

Date		Explanation	Post. Ref.	Debit	Credit	Balance

NAME:________________________

Comprehensive Problem 1 *(continued)*

Instructions 1, 3, 11 and 13

JEAN PIERRE DUBOIS, CAPITAL ACCT. NO. 310

Date		Explanation	Post. Ref.	Debit	Credit	Balance
20XX Oct.	1	Balance	✓			1488628 6

JEAN PIERRE DUBOIS, DRAWING ACCT. NO. 320

Date		Explanation	Post. Ref.	Debit	Credit	Balance

INCOME SUMMARY ACCT. NO. 330

Date		Explanation	Post. Ref.	Debit	Credit	Balance

REVENUE FROM SUBSCRIPTIONS ACCT. NO. 410

Date		Explanation	Post. Ref.	Debit	Credit	Balance

CONSULTING REVENUE ACCT. NO. 420

Date		Explanation	Post. Ref.	Debit	Credit	Balance

NAME:____________________

Comprehensive Problem 1 *(continued)*

Instructions 1, 3, 11 and 13

UTILITIES EXPENSE **ACCT. NO. 610**

Date		Explanation	Post. Ref.	Debit	Credit	Balance

WAGES EXPENSE **ACCT. NO. 620**

Date		Explanation	Post. Ref.	Debit	Credit	Balance

ADVERTISING EXPENSE **ACCT. NO. 630**

Date		Explanation	Post. Ref.	Debit	Credit	Balance

GASOLINE AND OIL EXPENSE **ACCT. NO. 640**

Date		Explanation	Post. Ref.	Debit	Credit	Balance

BUILDING REPAIRS EXPENSE **ACCT. NO. 650**

Date		Explanation	Post. Ref.	Debit	Credit	Balance

NAME:________________________

Comprehensive Problem 1 *(continued)*

Instructions 1, 3, 11 and 13

VAN REPAIRS EXPENSE — **ACCT. NO. 655**

Date		Explanation	Post. Ref.	Debit	Credit	Balance

INTEREST EXPENSE — **ACCT. NO. 660**

Date		Explanation	Post. Ref.	Debit	Credit	Balance

SUPPLIES EXPENSE — **ACCT. NO. 670**

Date		Explanation	Post. Ref.	Debit	Credit	Balance

INSURANCE EXPENSE — **ACCT. NO. 680**

Date		Explanation	Post. Ref.	Debit	Credit	Balance

AMORTIZATION EXPENSE — **ACCT. NO. 690**

Date		Explanation	Post. Ref.	Debit	Credit	Balance

Comprehensive Problem 1

NAME:______________________

Instructions 4, 5 and 6

Le Grand Journal					
Worksheet					
For the Month Ended October 31, 20XX					
Acct. No.	Account Title	Unadjusted Trial Balance		Adjustments	
		Debit	Credit	Debit	Credit
110	Cash	15680 82			
120	Accounts Receivable	12781 37			
130	Supplies	3922 22			
135	Prepaid Insurance	600 —			
138	Land	36000 —			
140	Equipment	75000 —			
141	Acc. Amortization – Equipment		19800 —		
150	Delivery Van	21640 —			
151	Acc. Amortization – Delivery Van		10800 —		
160	Furniture	4300 —			
161	Acc. Amortization – Furniture		2145 —		
170	Building	195000 —			
171	Acc. Amortization – Building		24750 —		
210	Accounts Payable		5193 32		
220	Notes Payable		31308 06		
225	Unearned Consulting Revenue		1000 —		
230	Mortgage Payable – Building		121879 60		
240	Wages Payable				
310	J.P. Dubois, Capital		148862 86		
320	J.P. Dubois, Drawing	6000 00			
410	Revenue from Subscriptions		21043 80		
420	Consulting Revenue				
610	Utilities Expense	946 23			
620	Wages Expense	6821 54			
630	Advertising Expense	3412 90			
640	Gas & Oil Expense	576 24			
650	Building Repairs Expense	2003 50			
655	Van Repairs Expense	217 40			
660	Interest Expense	1880 42			
	Totals	386782 64	386782 64		
670	Supplies Expense				
680	Insurance Expense				
690	Amortization Expense				
	Totals				

Comprehensive Problem 1 *(continued)* NAME:______________________________

Instructions 4, 5 and 6

Adjusted Trial Balance		Income Statement		Balance Sheet	
Debit	Credit	Debit	Credit	Debit	Credit

NAME:________________________

Comprehensive Problem 1 *(continued)*

Instruction 7

NAME:________________

Comprehensive Problem 1 *(continued)*

Instruction 8

Comprehensive Problem 1 *(continued)*

NAME:________________________

Instruction 9

NAME:______________________

Comprehensive Problem 1 *(continued)*

Instruction 14

____

____

____

NAME: ______________________

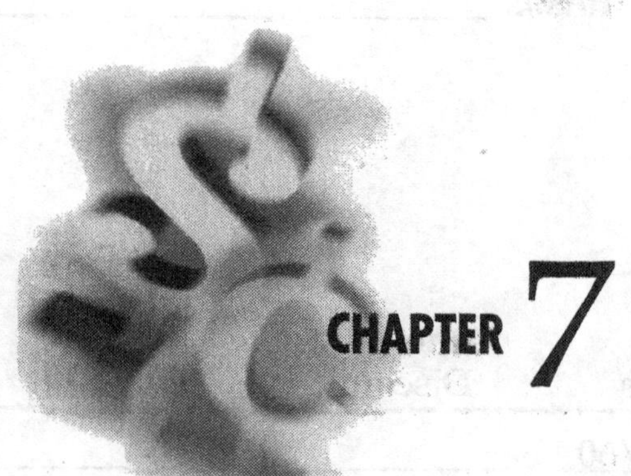

CHAPTER 7

The Sales Journal and the Accounts Receivable Subsidiary Ledger

Vocabulary Review

1. ______________________
2. ______________________
3. ______________________
4. ______________________
5. ______________________
6. ______________________
7. ______________________
8. ______________________
9. ______________________
10. ______________________
11. ______________________
12. ______________________
13. ______________________
14. ______________________
15. ______________________
16. ______________________
17. ______________________
18. ______________________
19. ______________________
20. ______________________
21. ______________________
22. ______________________
23. ______________________
24. ______________________
25. ______________________
26. ______________________
27. ______________________
28. ______________________
29. ______________________
30. ______________________
31. ______________________
32. ______________________
33. ______________________
34. ______________________
35. ______________________
36. ______________________

NAME:________________________

Exercise 7.1

	Invoice Amount	Invoice Date	Terms	Amount of Discount	Last Day to Pay and Receive Discount
a.	$ 1,200	January 26	1/15, n/60		
b.	3,780	March 22	2/10, n/30		
c.	10,460	June 20	2/15, n/30		
d.	475	July 29	1/10, n/60		
e.	520	August 30	2/15, n/60		
f.	1,650	September 30	2/10, n/30		
g.	5,720	November 16	1/15, n/60		
h.	15,240	October 19	2/15, n/60		

NAME:______________________________

Exercise 7.2

GENERAL JOURNAL			PAGE NO.	
Date	Description	Post. Ref.	Debit	Credit

NAME:________________________

Exercise 7.2 *(continued)*

GENERAL LEDGER

CASH **ACCT. NO. 101**

Date		Explanation	Post. Ref.	Debit	Credit	Balance

ACCOUNTS RECEIVABLE **ACCT. NO. 110**

Date		Explanation	Post. Ref.	Debit	Credit	Balance

PROVINCIAL SALES TAX PAYABLE **ACCT. NO. 210**

Date		Explanation	Post. Ref.	Debit	Credit	Balance

GST PAYABLE **ACCT. NO. 230**

Date		Explanation	Post. Ref.	Debit	Credit	Balance

SALES **ACCT. NO. 405**

Date		Explanation	Post. Ref.	Debit	Credit	Balance

SALES RETURNS AND ALLOWANCES **ACCT. NO. 410**

Date		Explanation	Post. Ref.	Debit	Credit	Balance

NAME:______________________________

Exercise 7.2 *(continued)*

ACCOUNTS RECEIVABLE SUBSIDIARY LEDGER

MERINO, ROGER

Date		Explanation	Post. Ref.	Debit	Credit	Balance

Exercise 7.3

GENERAL JOURNAL				PAGE NO.	
Date		Description	Post. Ref.	Debit	Credit

NAME:_______________________

Exercise 7.3 *(continued)*

GENERAL LEDGER

CASH **ACCT. NO. 101**

Date		Explanation	Post. Ref.	Debit	Credit	Balance

ACCOUNTS RECEIVABLE **ACCT. NO. 110**

Date		Explanation	Post. Ref.	Debit	Credit	Balance

GST PAYABLE **ACCT. NO. 235**

Date		Explanation	Post. Ref.	Debit	Credit	Balance

SALES **ACCT. NO. 401**

Date		Explanation	Post. Ref.	Debit	Credit	Balance

SALES RETURNS AND ALLOWANCES **ACCT. NO. 405**

Date		Explanation	Post. Ref.	Debit	Credit	Balance

SALES DISCOUNTS **ACCT. NO. 410**

Date		Explanation	Post. Ref.	Debit	Credit	Balance

NAME:____________________

Exercise 7.3 *(continued)*

ACCOUNTS RECEIVABLE SUBSIDIARY LEDGER

WATERBEDS GALORE

Date		Explanation	Post. Ref.	Debit	Credit	Balance

Exercise 7.4

a. ____________________

____

b. ____________________

____

c. ____________________

____

d. ____________________

____

NAME:____________________

Exercise 7.5

a.

b.

c.

d.

e.

f.

NAME:____________________

Exercise 7.6

____

____

____

Exercise 7.7

ACCOUNTS RECEIVABLE SUBSIDIARY LEDGER

BUG REPAIR SHOP

Date		Explanation	Post. Ref.	Debit	Credit	Balance
20XX Mar.	1		S3	870—		
	11		CR4		400—	
	15		S4	550—		
	19		GJ5		150—	

FOREIGN AUTO REPAIR

Date		Explanation	Post. Ref.	Debit	Credit	Balance
20XX Mar.	12		S4	65—		
	14		S4	170—		
	15		GJ5		40—	

NAME:____________________

Exercise 7.7 *(continued)*

JOANNA GRIMM

Date		Explanation	Post. Ref.	Debit	Credit	Balance
20XX Mar.	15		S4	375 —		
	25		CR4		375 —	
	28		S4	425 —		
	31		GJ6		125 —	

KURT ZANDER

Date		Explanation	Post. Ref.	Debit	Credit	Balance
20XX Mar.	20		S4	206 —		
	24		S4	115 —		
	25		S4	65 —		
	26		GJ6		65 —	
	30		CR4		206 —	

NAME: ____________________

Exercise 7.8

SALES JOURNAL								PAGE 7
Date		Sales Invoice Number	Customer's Name	Post. Ref.	Accounts Receivable Debit	PST Payable Credit	GST Payable Credit	Sales Credit
20XX May	3	305	R. Joyce	✓				240.00
	7	306	L. Hemming	✓				780.00
	11	307	T. Ayotte	✓				1215.00
	15	308	F. Brooks	✓				84.00
	23	309	L. Lyons	✓				530.00
	31	310	C. Little	✓				1920.00
	31	311	N. Thomas	✓				230.00
			Totals					

NAME:____________________

Problem 7.1

Instructions 2, 3 and 5

SALES JOURNAL							PAGE
Date	Sales Invoice Number	Customer's Name	Post. Ref.	Accounts Receivable Debit	PST Payable Credit	GST Payable Credit	Sales Credit

NAME:___________________________

Problem 7.1 *(continued)*

Instructions 2 and 3

GENERAL JOURNAL — PAGE NO.

Date		Description	Post. Ref.	Debit	Credit

NAME:______________________

Problem 7.1 *(continued)*

Instructions 1 and 6

GENERAL LEDGER

ACCOUNTS RECEIVABLE — ACCT. NO. 110

Date		Explanation	Post. Ref.	Debit	Credit	Balance
20XX Mar.	1	Balance Forward	✓			1005—

GST PAYABLE — ACCT. NO. 205

Date		Explanation	Post. Ref.	Debit	Credit	Balance

SALES — ACCT. NO. 400

Date		Explanation	Post. Ref.	Debit	Credit	Balance

SALES RETURNS AND ALLOWANCES — ACCT. NO. 410

Date		Explanation	Post. Ref.	Debit	Credit	Balance

NAME:______________________________

Problem 7.1 *(continued)*

Instructions 1 and 4

ACCOUNTS RECEIVABLE SUBSIDIARY LEDGER

ANGUS ACRES

Date		Explanation	Post. Ref.	Debit	Credit	Balance
20XX Mar.	1	Balance Forward	✓			250—

BAR-D RANCH

Date		Explanation	Post. Ref.	Debit	Credit	Balance
20XX Mar.	1	Balance Forward	✓			175—

OAK HILL RANCH

Date		Explanation	Post. Ref.	Debit	Credit	Balance
20XX Mar.	1	Balance Forward	✓			460—

SLEEPY RIVER RANCH

Date		Explanation	Post. Ref.	Debit	Credit	Balance
20XX Mar.	1	Balance Forward	✓			120—

NAME: ____________________

Problem 7.1 *(continued)*

Instruction 7

Problem 7.2

Instructions 2, 3 and 5

SALES JOURNAL							PAGE
Date	Sales Invoice Number	Customer's Name	Post. Ref.	Accounts Receivable Debit	PST Payable Credit	GST Payable Credit	Sales Credit

NAME:________________________

Problem 7.2 *(continued)*

Instructions 2 and 3

GENERAL JOURNAL PAGE NO.

Date		Description	Post. Ref.	Debit	Credit

NAME:________________________

Problem 7.2 *(continued)*

Instructions 1 and 6

GENERAL LEDGER

ACCOUNTS RECEIVABLE **ACCT. NO. 110**

Date		Explanation	Post. Ref.	Debit	Credit	Balance
20XX June	1	Balance Forward	✓			1980—

GST PAYABLE **ACCT. NO. 205**

Date		Explanation	Post. Ref.	Debit	Credit	Balance

SALES **ACCT. NO. 401**

Date		Explanation	Post. Ref.	Debit	Credit	Balance

SALES RETURNS AND ALLOWANCES **ACCT. NO. 410**

Date		Explanation	Post. Ref.	Debit	Credit	Balance

NAME:________________________

Problem 7.2 *(continued)*

Instructions 1 and 4

ACCOUNTS RECEIVABLE SUBSIDIARY LEDGER

APCO

Date		Explanation	Post. Ref.	Debit	Credit	Balance
20XX June	1	Balance Forward	✓			650 —

BESTCO

Date		Explanation	Post. Ref.	Debit	Credit	Balance
20XX June	1	Balance Forward	✓			490 —

BUY 'N SAVE

Date		Explanation	Post. Ref.	Debit	Credit	Balance
20XX June	1	Balance Forward	✓			840 —

NAME:____________________

Problem 7.2 *(continued)*

Instruction 7

____

____

____

Problem 7.3

Instructions 2, 3 and 5

SALES JOURNAL								PAGE
Date		Sales Invoice Number	Customer's Name	Post. Ref.	Accounts Receivable Debit	PST Payable Credit	GST Payable Credit	Sales Credit

NAME:__________________________

Problem 7.3 *(continued)*

Instructions 2 and 3

GENERAL JOURNAL — **PAGE NO.**

Date		Description	Post. Ref.	Debit	Credit

NAME:______________________

Problem 7.3 *(continued)*

Instructions 1 and 6

GENERAL LEDGER

ACCOUNTS RECEIVABLE — **ACCT. NO. 110**

Date 20XX		Explanation	Post. Ref.	Debit	Credit	Balance
Aug.	1	Balance Forward	✓			500 —

PROVINCIAL SALES TAX PAYABLE — **ACCT. NO. 210**

Date 20XX		Explanation	Post. Ref.	Debit	Credit	Balance
Aug.	1	Balance Forward	✓			120 —

GST PAYABLE — **ACCT. NO. 230**

Date 20XX		Explanation	Post. Ref.	Debit	Credit	Balance
Aug.	1	Balance Forward	✓			105 —

NAME:____________________

Problem 7.3 *(continued)*

Instruction 1 and 6

SALES **ACCT. NO. 410**

Date		Explanation	Post. Ref.	Debit	Credit	Balance

SALES RETURNS AND ALLOWANCES **ACCT. NO. 420**

Date		Explanation	Post. Ref.	Debit	Credit	Balance

Instructions 1 and 4

ACCOUNTS RECEIVABLE SUBSIDIARY LEDGER

JOHNSON, ANDY

Date		Explanation	Post. Ref.	Debit	Credit	Balance
20XX Aug.	1	Balance Forward	✓			125—

KEENE, GEORGIA

Date		Explanation	Post. Ref.	Debit	Credit	Balance
20XX Aug.	1	Balance Forward	✓			80—

NAME:____________________________

Problem 7.3 *(continued)*

METZINGER, BYRON

Date		Explanation	Post. Ref.	Debit	Credit	Balance
20XX Aug.	1	Balance Forward	✓			240 —

NAGASAKI, JOE

Date		Explanation	Post. Ref.	Debit	Credit	Balance
20XX Aug.	1	Balance Forward	✓			55 —

Instruction 7

____

____

____

NAME:______________________________

Problem 7.4

Instructions 2, 3 and 5

SALES JOURNAL							PAGE
Date	Sales Invoice Number	Customer's Name	Post. Ref.	Accounts Receivable Debit	PST Payable Credit	GST Payable Credit	Sales Credit

NAME:______________________

Problem 7.4 *(continued)*

Instructions 2 and 3

GENERAL JOURNAL PAGE NO.

Date		Description	Post. Ref.	Debit	Credit

NAME:______________________

Problem 7.4 *(continued)*

Instructions 1 and 6

GENERAL LEDGER

CASH ACCT. NO. 101

Date		Explanation	Post. Ref.	Debit	Credit	Balance
20XX May	1	Balance Forward	✓			4620—

ACCOUNTS RECEIVABLE ACCT. NO. 110

Date		Explanation	Post. Ref.	Debit	Credit	Balance

GST PAYABLE ACCT. NO. 235

Date		Explanation	Post. Ref.	Debit	Credit	Balance

SALES ACCT. NO. 401

Date		Explanation	Post. Ref.	Debit	Credit	Balance

SALES DISCOUNTS ACCT. NO. 406

Date		Explanation	Post. Ref.	Debit	Credit	Balance

NAME:______________________

Problem 7.4 *(continued)*

SALES RETURNS AND ALLOWANCES — **ACCT. NO. 411**

Date		Explanation	Post. Ref.	Debit	Credit	Balance

Instructions 1 and 4

ACCOUNTS RECEIVABLE SUBSIDIARY LEDGER

CHAIRS, INC.

Date		Explanation	Post. Ref.	Debit	Credit	Balance

HOUSE OF MAPLE

Date		Explanation	Post. Ref.	Debit	Credit	Balance

KITCHEN KORNER

Date		Explanation	Post. Ref.	Debit	Credit	Balance

MACK'S BAR STOOLS

Date		Explanation	Post. Ref.	Debit	Credit	Balance

NAME:____________________

Problem 7.4 *(continued)*

Instruction 7

____

____

____

Problem 7.5

Instructions 2, 3 and 5

SALES JOURNAL							PAGE
Date	Sales Invoice Number	Customer's Name	Post. Ref.	Accounts Receivable Debit	PST Payable Credit	GST Payable Credit	Sales Credit

NAME:____________________

Problem 7.5 *(continued)*

Instructions 1 and 3

GENERAL JOURNAL				PAGE NO.
Date	Description	Post. Ref.	Debit	Credit

NAME:________________________

Problem 7.5 *(continued)*

GENERAL JOURNAL				PAGE NO.	
Date		Description	Post. Ref.	Debit	Credit

NAME:________________________

Problem 7.5 *(continued)*

Instructions 1 and 6

GENERAL LEDGER

CASH — **ACCT. NO. 101**

Date		Explanation	Post. Ref.	Debit	Credit	Balance
20XX Nov.	1	Balance Forward	✓			3740 —

ACCOUNTS RECEIVABLE — **ACCT. NO. 110**

Date		Explanation	Post. Ref.	Debit	Credit	Balance

PROVINCIAL SALES TAX PAYABLE — **ACCT. NO. 210**

Date		Explanation	Post. Ref.	Debit	Credit	Balance

NAME:____________________

Problem 7.5 *(continued)*

GST PAYABLE — **ACCT. NO. 215**

Date		Explanation	Post. Ref.	Debit	Credit	Balance

SALES — **ACCT. NO. 401**

Date		Explanation	Post. Ref.	Debit	Credit	Balance

SALES DISCOUNTS — **ACCT. NO. 405**

Date		Explanation	Post. Ref.	Debit	Credit	Balance

SALES RETURNS AND ALLOWANCES — **ACCT. NO. 410**

Date		Explanation	Post. Ref.	Debit	Credit	Balance

NAME:______________________________

Problem 7.5 *(continued)*

Instructions 1 and 4

ACCOUNTS RECEIVABLE SUBSIDIARY LEDGER

BRUINING, LYNDA

Date		Explanation	Post. Ref.	Debit	Credit	Balance

HARRIS, JANA

Date		Explanation	Post. Ref.	Debit	Credit	Balance

LADOUCEUR, GABRIELLE

Date		Explanation	Post. Ref.	Debit	Credit	Balance

VERNON, DENISE

Date		Explanation	Post. Ref.	Debit	Credit	Balance

NAME:________________________

Problem 7.5

Instruction 7

____

____

____

NAME: ____________________

CHAPTER 8

The Purchases Journal and the Accounts Payable Subsidiary Ledger

Vocabulary Review

1. ____________________
2. ____________________
3. ____________________
4. ____________________
5. ____________________
6. ____________________
7. ____________________
8. ____________________
9. ____________________
10. ____________________
11. ____________________
12. ____________________
13. ____________________
14. ____________________
15. ____________________
16. ____________________
17. ____________________
18. ____________________
19. ____________________
20. ____________________
21. ____________________
22. ____________________
23. ____________________
24. ____________________
25. ____________________
26. ____________________
27. ____________________
28. ____________________
29. ____________________
30. ____________________

NAME:________________________

Exercise 8.1

	Invoice amount	Invoice date	Terms	Last day for discount	Last day for payment after discount	Amount of discount
a.	$ 1,000	January 18	1/15, n/60			
b.	4,750	February 20	2/10, EOM			
c.	500	April 25	2/10, n/30			
d.	8,040	June 27	1/15, n/30			
e.	3,000	July 29	60 days			
f.	5,500	September 11	2/10, n/60			
g.	7,420	November 21	1/15, n/60			
h.	9,000	December 14	1/10, EOM			

NAME:________________________

Exercise 8.2

PURCHASES JOURNAL						PAGE
Date	Supplier's Name	Invoice Number	Post. Ref.	Purchases Debit	GST Refundable Debit	Accounts Payable Credit

GENERAL JOURNAL				PAGE NO.
Date	Description	Post. Ref.	Debit	Credit

NAME:______________________

Exercise 8.3

SALES JOURNAL							PAGE
Date	Sales Invoice Number	Customer's Name	Post. Ref.	Accounts Receivable Debit	PST Payable Credit	GST Payable Credit	Sales Credit

GENERAL JOURNAL				PAGE NO.
Date	Description	Post. Ref.	Debit	Credit

NAME:________________________________

Exercise 8.4

PURCHASES JOURNAL							PAGE
Date		Supplier's Name	Invoice Number	Post. Ref.	Purchases Debit	GST Refundable Debit	Accounts Payable Credit

GENERAL JOURNAL					PAGE NO.
Date		Description	Post. Ref.	Debit	Credit

NAME:________________________

Exercise 8.5

SALES JOURNAL							PAGE
Date	Sales Invoice Number	Customer's Name	Post. Ref.	Accounts Receivable Debit	PST Payable Credit	GST Payable Credit	Sales Credit

GENERAL JOURNAL			PAGE NO.	
Date	Description	Post. Ref.	Debit	Credit

NAME:

Exercise 8.6

August 10

August 10

August 12

August 20

Exercise 8.7

a.

b.

c.

d.

NAME: ______________________

Exercise 8.8

____

____

____

____

____

____

Exercise 8.9

ACCOUNTS PAYABLE SUBSIDIARY LEDGER

ALL-WEATHER COATS

Date		Explanation	Post. Ref.	Debit	Credit	Balance
20XX Aug.	1		P8		500—	
	3		GJ10	150—		
	5		P9		700—	
	11		CP14	350—		

CANVAS CLOTHES

Date		Explanation	Post. Ref.	Debit	Credit	Balance
20XX Aug.	4		P8		250—	
	9		P8		460—	
	10		GJ10	100—		
	14		CP14	150—		
	20		P8		300—	

NAME: ____________________

Exercise 8.9 *(continued)*

KIDDIE KORNER

Date		Explanation	Post. Ref.	Debit	Credit	Balance
20XX Aug.	7		P8		260—	
	9		P8		410—	
	10		P8		520—	
	17		CP14	260—		

LITTLE MEN

Date		Explanation	Post. Ref.	Debit	Credit	Balance
20XX Aug.	15		P8		305—	
	16		GJ10	305—		
	17		P8		420—	
	27		CP14	420—		
	31		P8		505—	

____

____

____

NAME:______________________

Exercise 8.10

Account Title	Account Classification	Normal Debit or Credit Balance	Which Financial Statement?
Example: Accumulated Amortization	Contra Asset	Credit	Balance Sheet
a. Mortgage Payable			
b. Sales			
c. Unearned Revenue			
d. Supplies Expense			
e. GST Payable			
f. Purchases Discounts			
g. Freight In			
h. Amortization Expense			
i. Purchases Returns & Allowances			
j. GST Refundable			
k. Prepaid Advertising			
l. Supplies			
m. Provincial Sales Tax Payable			
n. Merchandise Inventory			
o. Accounts Receivable			
p. Drawing			
q. Sales Returns and Allowances			
r. Prepaid Insurance			
s. Sales Discounts			

NAME:______________________________

Problem 8.1

Instructions 2 and 3

PURCHASES JOURNAL						PAGE
Date	Supplier's Name	Invoice Number	Post. Ref.	Purchases Debit	GST Refundable Debit	Accounts Payable Credit

NAME:____________________

Problem 8.1 *(continued)*

Instructions 2 and 3

GENERAL JOURNAL PAGE NO.

Date		Description	Post. Ref.	Debit	Credit

NAME:________________________

Problem 8.1 *(continued)*

Instructions 1 and 5

GENERAL LEDGER

CASH **ACCT. NO. 101**

Date		Explanation	Post. Ref.	Debit	Credit	Balance
20XX May	1	Balance Forward	✓			8700—

ACCOUNTS PAYABLE **ACCT. NO. 210**

Date		Explanation	Post. Ref.	Debit	Credit	Balance
20XX May	1	Balance Forward	✓			7600—

GST REFUNDABLE **ACCT. NO. 220**

Date		Explanation	Post. Ref.	Debit	Credit	Balance
20XX May	1	Balance Forward	✓			500—

PURCHASES **ACCT. NO. 511**

Date		Explanation	Post. Ref.	Debit	Credit	Balance

NAME:________________________

Problem 8.1 *(continued)*

Instructions 1 and 5

PURCHASES RETURNS AND ALLOWANCES — **ACCT. NO. 515**

Date		Explanation	Post. Ref.	Debit	Credit	Balance

Instructions 1 and 4

ACCOUNTS PAYABLE SUBSIDIARY LEDGER

GOLD PRODUCTS CO.

Date		Explanation	Post. Ref.	Debit	Credit	Balance

M & M JEWELLERY

Date		Explanation	Post. Ref.	Debit	Credit	Balance
20XX May	1	Balance Forward	✓			2000—

RICH'S SUPPLIES

Date		Explanation	Post. Ref.	Debit	Credit	Balance
20XX May	1	Balance Forward	✓			4500—

RING WAREHOUSE

Date		Explanation	Post. Ref.	Debit	Credit	Balance

NAME:______________________________

Problem 8.1 *(continued)*

SILVER SUPPLIES

Date		Explanation	Post. Ref.	Debit	Credit	Balance
20XX May	1	Balance Forward	✓			1100—

Instruction 6

____

____

____

NAME:______________________________

Problem 8.2

Instructions 2 and 3

PURCHASES JOURNAL							PAGE
Date		Supplier's Name	Invoice Number	Post. Ref.	Purchases Debit	GST Refundable Debit	Accounts Payable Credit

NAME:________________________

Problem 8.2 *(continued)*

Instructions 2 and 3

GENERAL JOURNAL			PAGE NO.	
Date	Description	Post. Ref.	Debit	Credit

NAME:________________

Problem 8.2 *(continued)*

Instructions 1 and 5

GENERAL LEDGER

CASH — **ACCT. NO. 101**

Date 20XX		Explanation	Post. Ref.	Debit	Credit	Balance
Feb.	1	Balance Forward	✓			7230 —

ACCOUNTS PAYABLE — **ACCT. NO. 211**

Date 20XX		Explanation	Post. Ref.	Debit	Credit	Balance
Feb.	1	Balance Forward	✓			6430 —

GST REFUNDABLE — **ACCT. NO. 220**

Date 20XX		Explanation	Post. Ref.	Debit	Credit	Balance
Feb.	1	Balance Forward	✓			420 —

NAME: ____________________

Problem 8.2 *(continued)*

Instructions 1 and 5

PURCHASES **ACCT. NO. 511**

Date		Explanation	Post. Ref.	Debit	Credit	Balance

PURCHASES RETURNS AND ALLOWANCES **ACCT. NO. 515**

Date		Explanation	Post. Ref.	Debit	Credit	Balance

PURCHASES DISCOUNTS **ACCT. NO. 520**

Date		Explanation	Post. Ref.	Debit	Credit	Balance

Instructions 1 and 4

ACCOUNTS PAYABLE SUBSIDIARY LEDGER

COWHAND SUPPLIES

Date		Explanation	Post. Ref.	Debit	Credit	Balance
20XX Feb.	1	Balance Forward	✓			3000—

NAME:____________________

Problem 8.2 *(continued)*

Instructions 1 and 4

DOUBLE R SUPPLIES

Date		Explanation	Post. Ref.	Debit	Credit	Balance
20XX Feb.	1	Balance Forward	✓			2000—

LEATHER PRODUCTS

Date		Explanation	Post. Ref.	Debit	Credit	Balance
20XX Feb.	1	Balance Forward	✓			1430—

RINGO WESTERN WEAR

Date		Explanation	Post. Ref.	Debit	Credit	Balance

Instructions 6

____

____

____

NAME:

Problem 8.3

Instructions 2 and 3

PURCHASES JOURNAL							PAGE
Date		Supplier's Name	Invoice Number	Post. Ref.	Purchases Debit	GST Refundable Debit	Accounts Payable Credit

NAME:______________________

Problem 8.3 *(continued)*

Instructions 2 and 3

GENERAL JOURNAL			PAGE NO.	
Date	Description	Post. Ref.	Debit	Credit

NAME:________________________

Problem 8.3 *(continued)*

Instructions 2 and 3

GENERAL JOURNAL — **PAGE NO.**

Date		Description	Post. Ref.	Debit	Credit

NAME:______________________

Problem 8.3 *(continued)*

Instructions 1 and 5

GENERAL LEDGER

CASH **ACCT. NO. 101**

Date		Explanation	Post. Ref.	Debit	Credit	Balance
20XX Jan.	1	Balance Forward	✓			16100—

ACCOUNTS PAYABLE **ACCT. NO. 211**

Date		Explanation	Post. Ref.	Debit	Credit	Balance
20XX Jan.	1	Balance Forward	✓			8900—

GST REFUNDABLE **ACCT. NO. 230**

Date		Explanation	Post. Ref.	Debit	Credit	Balance
20XX Jan.	1	Balance Forward	✓			580—

NAME:___________________________

Problem 8.3 *(continued)*

Instructions 1 and 5

PURCHASES — **ACCT. NO. 501**

Date		Explanation	Post. Ref.	Debit	Credit	Balance

PURCHASES RETURNS AND ALLOWANCES — **ACCT. NO. 510**

Date		Explanation	Post. Ref.	Debit	Credit	Balance

PURCHASES DISCOUNTS — **ACCT. NO. 520**

Date		Explanation	Post. Ref.	Debit	Credit	Balance

FREIGHT IN — **ACCT. NO. 525**

Date		Explanation	Post. Ref.	Debit	Credit	Balance

NAME:______________________

Problem 8.3 *(continued)*

Instructions 1 and 4

ACCOUNTS PAYABLE SUBSIDIARY LEDGER

A-1 PRODUCTS

Date		Explanation	Post. Ref.	Debit	Credit	Balance
20XX Jan.	1	Balance Forward	✓			3000—

BARGAIN BASEMENT

Date		Explanation	Post. Ref.	Debit	Credit	Balance
20XX Jan.	1	Balance Forward	✓			2500—

BEST PRODUCTS

Date		Explanation	Post. Ref.	Debit	Credit	Balance

KLEAN HOMES

Date		Explanation	Post. Ref.	Debit	Credit	Balance
20XX Jan.	1	Balance Forward	✓			2000—

NAME:____________________

Problem 8.3 *(continued)*

Instructions 1 and 4

ZUMWALT'S

Date		Explanation	Post. Ref.	Debit	Credit	Balance
20XX Jan.	1	Balance Forward	✓			1400—

Instruction 6

____

____

____

NAME:________________________

Problem 8.4

Instruction 3

SALES JOURNAL								PAGE
Date		Sales Invoice Number	Customer's Name	Post. Ref.	Accounts Receivable Debit	PST Payable Credit	GST Payable Credit	Sales Credit

PURCHASES JOURNAL							PAGE
Date		Supplier's Name	Invoice Number	Post. Ref.	Purchases Debit	GST Refundable Debit	Accounts Payable Credit

NAME:________________________

Problem 8.4 *(continued)*

Instruction 3

GENERAL JOURNAL				PAGE NO.	
Date		Description	Post. Ref.	Debit	Credit

NAME:______________________________

Problem 8.4 *(continued)*

Instruction 3

GENERAL JOURNAL			PAGE NO.	
Date	Description	Post. Ref.	Debit	Credit

NAME:_______________

Problem 8.4 *(continued)*

Instructions 2 and 3a

ACCOUNTS RECEIVABLE SUBSIDIARY LEDGER

B. L. BOTHAM

Date		Explanation	Post. Ref.	Debit	Credit	Balance

THE SEWING CORNER

Date		Explanation	Post. Ref.	Debit	Credit	Balance

ACCOUNTS PAYABLE SUBSIDIARY LEDGER

G & B FABRICS

Date		Explanation	Post. Ref.	Debit	Credit	Balance

KATHY'S SEWRIGHT MACHINES

Date		Explanation	Post. Ref.	Debit	Credit	Balance

KWIK-SEW

Date		Explanation	Post. Ref.	Debit	Credit	Balance

NAME:________________________________

Problem 8.5

Instructions 3 and 4

SALES JOURNAL							PAGE
Date	Sales Invoice Number	Customer's Name	Post. Ref.	Accounts Receivable Debit	PST Payable Credit	GST Payable Credit	Sales Credit

PURCHASES JOURNAL						PAGE
Date	Supplier's Name	Invoice Number	Post. Ref.	Purchases Debit	GST Refundable Debit	Accounts Payable Credit

NAME:

Problem 8.5 *(continued)*

Instruction 3

GENERAL JOURNAL			PAGE NO.	
Date	Description	Post. Ref.	Debit	Credit

NAME:________________________

Problem 8.5 *(continued)*

Instruction 3

GENERAL JOURNAL PAGE NO.

Date	Description	Post. Ref.	Debit	Credit

NAME:______________________

Problem 8.5 *(continued)*

Instructions 2 and 5

ACCOUNTS RECEIVABLE SUBSIDIARY LEDGER

ROGERS, A.G.

Date		Explanation	Post. Ref.	Debit	Credit	Balance

TOLSTOY, P.S.

Date		Explanation	Post. Ref.	Debit	Credit	Balance

ULRICH, B.B.

Date		Explanation	Post. Ref.	Debit	Credit	Balance

ACCOUNTS PAYABLE SUBSIDIARY LEDGER

MORENO'S APPLIANCES

Date		Explanation	Post. Ref.	Debit	Credit	Balance

NAME:______________________

Problem 8.5 *(continued)*

Instructions 2 and 5

ACCOUNTS PAYABLE SUBSIDIARY LEDGER (continued)

VAN RIPER WHOLESALE HOUSE

Date		Explanation	Post. Ref.	Debit	Credit	Balance

WILSON SUPPLIES

Date		Explanation	Post. Ref.	Debit	Credit	Balance

NAME: ______________________

CHAPTER 9

The Cash Receipts, Cash Payments, and Combined Cash Journals

Vocabulary Review

1. ______________________
2. ______________________
3. ______________________
4. ______________________
5. ______________________
6. ______________________
7. ______________________
8. ______________________
9. ______________________
10. ______________________
11. ______________________
12. ______________________
13. ______________________
14. ______________________
15. ______________________
16. ______________________
17. ______________________
18. ______________________
19. ______________________
20. ______________________
21. ______________________
22. ______________________
23. ______________________
24. ______________________
25. ______________________
26. ______________________
27. ______________________
28. ______________________
29. ______________________
30. ______________________
31. ______________________
32. ______________________
33. ______________________
34. ______________________

NAME:____________________

Exercise 9.1

GENERAL JOURNAL				PAGE NO.	
Date		Description	Post. Ref.	Debit	Credit

NAME:________________________________

Exercise 9.2

GENERAL JOURNAL				PAGE NO.	
Date		Description	Post. Ref.	Debit	Credit

NAME:________________________

Exercise 9.2 *(continued)*

GENERAL JOURNAL			PAGE NO.	
Date	Description	Post. Ref.	Debit	Credit

NAME:____________________

Exercise 9.3

	Interest	=	Principal	×	Rate	×	Time
a.							
b.							
c.							
d.							
e.							
f.							
g.							
h.							
i.							
j.							

Exercise 9.4

a.

b.

NAME:______________________________

Exercise 9.5

GENERAL JOURNAL			PAGE NO.	
Date	Description	Post. Ref.	Debit	Credit

NAME:______________________________

Exercise 9.6

GENERAL JOURNAL				PAGE NO.	
Date		Description	Post. Ref.	Debit	Credit

Exercise 9.7

GENERAL JOURNAL				PAGE NO.	
Date		Description	Post. Ref.	Debit	Credit

NAME:________________________

Exercise 9.8

		GENERAL JOURNAL		PAGE NO.	
Date		Description	Post. Ref.	Debit	Credit

NAME:______________________

Exercise 9.8 *(continued)*

Cash Short and Over

Exercise 9.9

a. ______________________

b. ______________________

c. ______________________

d. ______________________

e. ______________________

f. ______________________

g. ______________________

h. ______________________

i. ______________________

j. ______________________

k. ______________________

l. ______________________

m. ______________________

n. ______________________

o. ______________________

p. ______________________

q. ______________________

r. ______________________

s. ______________________

t. ______________________

NAME:

Problem 9.1

Instructions 1 and 2

CASH RECEIPTS JOURNAL									PAGE
Date	Received From	Account Credited	Post. Ref.	Sundry Accounts Credit	Accounts Receivable Credit	Sales Credit	GST Payable Credit	Credit Card Discount Debit	Cash Debit

NAME: ____________________

Problem 9.2

Instructions 1 and 2

CASH PAYMENTS JOURNAL									PAGE
Date	Cheque No.	Paid To	Account Debited	Post. Ref.	Sundry Accounts Debit	Purchases Debit	GST Refundable Debit	Purchases Discount Credit	Cash Credit

NAME:____________________

Problem 9.3

Instructions 2 and 4

CASH RECEIPTS JOURNAL									PAGE
Date	Received From	Account Credited	Post. Ref.	Sundry Accounts Credit	Accounts Receivable Credit	Sales Credit	GST Payable Credit	Credit Card Discount Debit	Cash Debit

NAME: ____________________

Problem 9.3 *(continued)*

Instructions 2 and 5

CASH PAYMENTS JOURNAL — PAGE

Date		Cheque No.	Account Debited	Post. Ref.	Sundry Accounts Debit	Accounts Payable Debit	Purchases Debit	GST Refundable Debit	Purchases Discounts Credit	Cash Credit

NAME:________________________

Problem 9.3 *(continued)*

Instructions 1, 4 and 6

GENERAL LEDGER

CASH — **ACCT. NO. 101**

Date		Explanation	Post. Ref.	Debit	Credit	Balance
20XX Dec.	1	Balance Forward	✓			3800—

ACCOUNTS RECEIVABLE — **ACCT. NO. 110**

Date		Explanation	Post. Ref.	Debit	Credit	Balance
20XX Dec.	1	Balance Forward	✓			5000—

NOTES RECEIVABLE — **ACCT. NO. 120**

Date		Explanation	Post. Ref.	Debit	Credit	Balance
20XX Dec.	1	Balance Forward	✓			400—

ACCOUNTS PAYABLE — **ACCT. NO. 201**

Date		Explanation	Post. Ref.	Debit	Credit	Balance
20XX Dec.	1	Balance Forward	✓			3000—

NOTES PAYABLE — **ACCT. NO. 210**

Date		Explanation	Post. Ref.	Debit	Credit	Balance
20XX Dec.	1	Balance Forward	✓			2500—

NAME:________________________

Problem 9.3 *(continued)*

Instructions 1, 4 and 6

GST PAYABLE — **ACCT. NO. 220**

Date		Explanation	Post. Ref.	Debit	Credit	Balance
20XX Dec.	1	Balance Forward	✓			600—

GST REFUNDABLE — **ACCT. NO. 230**

Date		Explanation	Post. Ref.	Debit	Credit	Balance
20XX Dec.	1	Balance Forward	✓			280—

GRACE O'BRIEN, CAPITAL — **ACCT. NO. 301**

Date		Explanation	Post. Ref.	Debit	Credit	Balance
20XX Dec.	1	Balance Forward	✓			7500—

GRACE O'BRIEN, DRAWING — **ACCT. NO. 310**

Date		Explanation	Post. Ref.	Debit	Credit	Balance

SALES — **ACCT. NO. 401**

Date		Explanation	Post. Ref.	Debit	Credit	Balance

INTEREST INCOME — **ACCT. NO. 410**

Date		Explanation	Post. Ref.	Debit	Credit	Balance

PURCHASES — **ACCT. NO. 501**

Date		Explanation	Post. Ref.	Debit	Credit	Balance

NAME:____________________

Problem 9.3 *(continued)*

Instructions 1, 4 and 6

PURCHASES DISCOUNTS — **ACCT. NO. 510**

Date		Explanation	Post. Ref.	Debit	Credit	Balance

CREDIT CARD DISCOUNT EXPENSE — **ACCT. NO. 601**

Date		Explanation	Post. Ref.	Debit	Credit	Balance

SALARIES EXPENSE — **ACCT. NO. 610**

Date		Explanation	Post. Ref.	Debit	Credit	Balance

UTILITIES EXPENSE — **ACCT. NO. 620**

Date		Explanation	Post. Ref.	Debit	Credit	Balance

RENT EXPENSE — **ACCT. NO. 630**

Date		Explanation	Post. Ref.	Debit	Credit	Balance

INTEREST EXPENSE — **ACCT. NO. 640**

Date		Explanation	Post. Ref.	Debit	Credit	Balance

NAME:________________________

Problem 9.3 *(continued)*

Instructions 1 and 3

ACCOUNTS RECEIVABLE SUBSIDIARY LEDGER

BROWN, ELLEN

Date		Explanation	Post. Ref.	Debit	Credit	Balance
20XX Dec.	1	Balance Forward	✓			150—

KONG, KENNETH

Date		Explanation	Post. Ref.	Debit	Credit	Balance
20XX Dec.	1	Balance Forward	✓			150—

WONDER CHARGE COMPANY

Date		Explanation	Post. Ref.	Debit	Credit	Balance
20XX Dec.	1	Balance Forward	✓			3531—

ACCOUNTS PAYABLE SUBSIDIARY LEDGER

BOOK WHOLESALERS

Date		Explanation	Post. Ref.	Debit	Credit	Balance
20XX Dec.	1	Balance Forward	✓			802 50

PAPERBACKS, INC.

Date		Explanation	Post. Ref.	Debit	Credit	Balance
20XX Dec.	1	Balance Forward	✓			963—

NAME:________________________

Problem 9.4

Instructions 2, 5 and 6

SALES JOURNAL PAGE

Date	Sales Invoice Number	Customer's Name	Post. Ref.	Accounts Receivable Debit	PST Payable Credit	GST Payable Credit	Sales Credit

PURCHASES JOURNAL PAGE

Date	Supplier's Name	Invoice Number	Post. Ref.	Purchases Debit	GST Refundable Debit	Accounts Payable Credit

NAME: ____________________

Problem 9.4 *(continued)*

Instructions 2, 5 and 6

CASH RECEIPTS JOURNAL — **PAGE**

Date		Received From	Account Credited	Post. Ref.	Sundry Accounts Credit	Accounts Receivable Credit	Sales Credit	GST Payable Credit	Credit Card Discount Debit	Cash Debit

NAME:

Problem 9.4 *(continued)*

Instructions 2, 5 and 6

CASH PAYMENTS JOURNAL — **PAGE**

Date	Cheque No.	Paid To	Account Debited	Post. Ref.	Sundry Accounts Debit	Purchases Debit	GST Refundable Debit	Purchases Discount Credit	Cash Credit

NAME:____________________

Problem 9.4

Instructions 1, 4 and 6

GENERAL LEDGER

CASH — ACCT. NO. 101

Date		Explanation	Post. Ref.	Debit	Credit	Balance
20XX May	1	Balance	✓			18650—

ACCOUNTS RECEIVABLE — ACCT. NO. 110

Date		Explanation	Post. Ref.	Debit	Credit	Balance
20XX May	1	Balance	✓			2040—

OFFICE EQUIPMENT — ACCT. NO. 130

Date		Explanation	Post. Ref.	Debit	Credit	Balance

ACCOUNTS PAYABLE — ACCT. NO. 210

Date		Explanation	Post. Ref.	Debit	Credit	Balance
20XX May	1	Balance	✓			1570—

NAME:______________________

Problem 9.4 *(continued)*

Instructions 1, 4 and 6 (continued)

GST PAYABLE — ACCT. NO. 220

Date		Explanation	Post. Ref.	Debit	Credit	Balance
20XX May	1	Balance	✓			2030—

GST REFUNDABLE — ACCT. NO. 230

Date		Explanation	Post. Ref.	Debit	Credit	Balance
20XX May	1	Balance	✓			1460—

J. DEKLERK, CAPITAL — ACCT. NO. 301

Date		Explanation	Post. Ref.	Debit	Credit	Balance
20XX May	1	Balance				16400—

J. DEKLERK, DRAWING — ACCT. NO. 310

Date		Explanation	Post. Ref.	Debit	Credit	Balance

SALES — ACCOUNT NO. 401

Date		Explanation	Post. Ref.	Debit	Credit	Balance

SALES RETURNS AND ALLOWANCES — ACCT. NO. 410

Date		Explanation	Post. Ref.	Debit	Credit	Balance

NAME:______________________________

Problem 9.4 *(continued)*

Instructions 1, 4 and 6 (continued)

PURCHASES **ACCOUNT NO. 501**

Date		Explanation	Post. Ref.	Debit	Credit	Balance

PURCHASES RETURNS AND ALLOWANCES **ACCT. NO. 510**

Date		Explanation	Post. Ref.	Debit	Credit	Balance

RENT EXPENSE **ACCT. NO. 601**

Date		Explanation	Post. Ref.	Debit	Credit	Balance

UTILITIES EXPENSE **ACCOUNT NO. 620**

Date		Explanation	Post. Ref.	Debit	Credit	Balance

CREDIT CARD DISCOUNT EXPENSE **ACCT. NO. 630**

Date		Explanation	Post. Ref.	Debit	Credit	Balance

NAME:________________________

Problem 9.4 *(continued)*

Instructions 1 and 3

ACCOUNTS RECEIVABLE SUBSIDIARY LEDGER

DOLE, BOB

Date		Explanation	Post. Ref.	Debit	Credit	Balance
20XX May	1	Balance	✓			400—

QUESNELLE, J.

Date		Explanation	Post. Ref.	Debit	Credit	Balance

SANTIAGO, R.

Date		Explanation	Post. Ref.	Debit	Credit	Balance

WIGGINS, H.

Date		Explanation	Post. Ref.	Debit	Credit	Balance

NAME:________________________

Problem 9.4 *(continued)*

Instructions 1 and 3

ACCOUNTS PAYABLE SUBSIDIARY LEDGER

BIKE WORLD

Date		Explanation	Post. Ref.	Debit	Credit	Balance

COMPUTER WORLD

Date		Explanation	Post. Ref.	Debit	Credit	Balance

CYCLE WORLD

Date		Explanation	Post. Ref.	Debit	Credit	Balance

THE CYCLERY

Date		Explanation	Post. Ref.	Debit	Credit	Balance

NAME:________________

Problem 9.4 *(continued)*

Instructions 2, 5 and 6

GENERAL JOURNAL			PAGE NO.	
Date	Description	Post. Ref.	Debit	Credit

NAME:____________________

Problem 9.5

Instructions 1 and 4

COMBINED CASH JOURNAL

Cash Debit	Cash Credit	GST Refundable Debit	GST Payable Credit	Date	Cheque Number	Account Titles and Explanations

NAME:________________________

Problem 9.5 *(continued)*

Instructions 1 and 4

PAGE

Post Ref.	Sundry		Accounts Receivable		Accounts Payable		Purchases Debit	Sales Credit	Invoice Number
	Debit	Credit	Debit	Credit	Debit	Credit			

NAME:________________________

Problem 9.5 *(continued)*

Instructions 3 and 5

GENERAL LEDGER

CASH **ACCT. NO. 101**

Date		Explanation	Post. Ref.	Debit	Credit	Balance

ACCOUNTS RECEIVABLE **ACCT. NO. 110**

Date		Explanation	Post. Ref.	Debit	Credit	Balance

ACCOUNTS PAYABLE **ACCT. NO. 210**

Date		Explanation	Post. Ref.	Debit	Credit	Balance

NOTES PAYABLE **ACCT. NO. 215**

Date		Explanation	Post. Ref.	Debit	Credit	Balance

GST PAYABLE **ACCT. NO. 220**

Date		Explanation	Post. Ref.	Debit	Credit	Balance

NAME:______________________

Problem 9.5 *(continued)*

Instructions 3 and 5

GST REFUNDABLE ACCT. NO. 230

Date		Explanation	Post. Ref.	Debit	Credit	Balance

JACK DANIELS, CAPITAL ACCT. NO. 310

Date		Explanation	Post. Ref.	Debit	Credit	Balance

JACK DANIELS, DRAWING ACCT. NO. 320

Date		Explanation	Post. Ref.	Debit	Credit	Balance

SALES ACCT. NO. 401

Date		Explanation	Post. Ref.	Debit	Credit	Balance

SALES RETURNS AND ALLOWANCES ACCT. NO. 410

Date		Explanation	Post. Ref.	Debit	Credit	Balance

PURCHASES ACCT. NO. 510

Date		Explanation	Post. Ref.	Debit	Credit	Balance

PURCHASES RETURNS AND ALLOWANCES ACCT. NO. 520

Date		Explanation	Post. Ref.	Debit	Credit	Balance

SALARIES EXPENSE ACCT. NO. 610

Date		Explanation	Post. Ref.	Debit	Credit	Balance

NAME:________________________

Problem 9.5 *(continued)*

Instructions 3 and 5

ADVERTISING EXPENSE — ACCT. NO. 620

Date		Explanation	Post. Ref.	Debit	Credit	Balance

RENT EXPENSE — ACCT. NO. 630

Date		Explanation	Post. Ref.	Debit	Credit	Balance

Instruction 2

ACCOUNTS RECEIVABLE SUBSIDIARY LEDGER

CREATIVE COOKERY

Date		Explanation	Post. Ref.	Debit	Credit	Balance

DAWSON DESIGNS

Date		Explanation	Post. Ref.	Debit	Credit	Balance

KRAFTY KITCHENS

Date		Explanation	Post. Ref.	Debit	Credit	Balance

NAME:__________________________

Problem 9.5 *(continued)*

Instruction 2

ACCOUNTS PAYABLE SUBSIDIARY LEDGER

ALLISTAR SUPPLIES

Date		Explanation	Post. Ref.	Debit	Credit	Balance

INTERNATIONAL IMPORTERS

Date		Explanation	Post. Ref.	Debit	Credit	Balance

KITCHEN KUPBOARDS

Date		Explanation	Post. Ref.	Debit	Credit	Balance

NAME:____________________

Problem 9.6

Instructions 1 and 4

COMBINED CASH JOURNAL

Cash Debit	Cash Credit	GST Refundable Debit	GST Payable Credit	Date	Cheque Number	Account Titles and Explanations

NAME:______________________

PAGE									
Post Ref.	Sundry		Accounts Receivable		Accounts Payable		Purchases Debit	Sales Credit	Invoice Number
	Debit	Credit	Debit	Credit	Debit	Credit			

NAME:________________________

Problem 9.6 *(continued)*

Instructions 3 and 5

GENERAL LEDGER

CASH — **ACCT. NO. 101**

Date		Explanation	Post. Ref.	Debit	Credit	Balance

ACCOUNTS RECEIVABLE — **ACCT. NO. 110**

Date		Explanation	Post. Ref.	Debit	Credit	Balance

OFFICE EQUIPMENT — **ACCT. NO. 120**

Date		Explanation	Post. Ref.	Debit	Credit	Balance

ACCOUNTS PAYABLE — **ACCT. NO. 210**

Date		Explanation	Post. Ref.	Debit	Credit	Balance

GST PAYABLE — **ACCT. NO. 220**

Date		Explanation	Post. Ref.	Debit	Credit	Balance

NAME:________________________

Problem 9.6 *(continued)*

Instructions 3 and 5

GST REFUNDABLE — ACCT. NO. 230

Date		Explanation	Post. Ref.	Debit	Credit	Balance

SALES — ACCT. NO. 401

Date		Explanation	Post. Ref.	Debit	Credit	Balance

SALES RETURNS AND ALLOWANCES — ACCT. NO. 410

Date		Explanation	Post. Ref.	Debit	Credit	Balance

SALES DISCOUNTS — ACCT. NO. 420

Date		Explanation	Post. Ref.	Debit	Credit	Balance

PURCHASES — ACCT. NO. 501

Date		Explanation	Post. Ref.	Debit	Credit	Balance

PURCHASES RETURNS AND ALLOWANCES — ACCT. NO. 510

Date		Explanation	Post. Ref.	Debit	Credit	Balance

PURCHASES DISCOUNTS — ACCT. NO. 520

Date		Explanation	Post. Ref.	Debit	Credit	Balance

NAME:____________________

Problem 9.6 *(continued)*

Instructions 3 and 5

RENT EXPENSE — **ACCT. NO. 620**

Date		Explanation	Post. Ref.	Debit	Credit	Balance

ADVERTISING EXPENSE — **ACCT. NO. 630**

Date		Explanation	Post. Ref.	Debit	Credit	Balance

Instruction 2

ACCOUNTS RECEIVABLE SUBSIDIARY LEDGER

LONG, TERRY

Date		Explanation	Post. Ref.	Debit	Credit	Balance

NASH, GERI

Date		Explanation	Post. Ref.	Debit	Credit	Balance

NAME:____________________________

Problem 9.6 *(continued)*

Instruction 2

ACCOUNTS PAYABLE SUBSIDIARY LEDGER

BESTCO COMPANY

Date		Explanation	Post. Ref.	Debit	Credit	Balance

GOODE COMPANY

Date		Explanation	Post. Ref.	Debit	Credit	Balance

WESTERN COMPANY

Date		Explanation	Post. Ref.	Debit	Credit	Balance

NAME: ______________________

CHAPTER 10

The Bank Account and Cash Funds

Vocabulary Review

1. ______________________
2. ______________________
3. ______________________
4. ______________________
5. ______________________
6. ______________________
7. ______________________
8. ______________________
9. ______________________
10. ______________________
11. ______________________
12. ______________________
13. ______________________
14. ______________________
15. ______________________
16. ______________________
17. ______________________
18. ______________________
19. ______________________
20. ______________________
21. ______________________
22. ______________________
23. ______________________
24. ______________________
25. ______________________
26. ______________________

NAME: ____________________

Exercise 10.1

CASH RECEIPTS JOURNAL PAGE

Date		Received From	Account Credited	Post. Ref.	Sundry Accounts Credit	Accounts Receivable Credit	Sales Credit	GST Payable Credit	Cash Short and Over Debit (Credit)	Cash Debit

DEPOSIT SLIP		
For deposit to the chequing account of MOM'S AUTO PARTS 14 River Blvd. Orangeville, ON L3V 7B7	CURRENCY	
	COIN	
	C	
	H	
20XX	E	
	Q	
	U	
	E	
	S	
TORONTO DOMINION BANK Main Street Orangeville, ON L7V 3B5	TOTAL	
	LESS CASH RECEIVED	
	NET DEPOSIT	

NAME:____________________

Exercise 10.2

Cash Short and Over

Exercise 10.3

a.

b.

c.

NAME:____________________

Exercise 10.4

GENERAL JOURNAL					PAGE NO.
Date		Description	Post. Ref.	Debit	Credit

NAME:________________________

Exercise 10.5

Exercise 10.6

NAME:________________________

Exercise 10.7

	Add To Bank Statement	Subtract From Bank Statement	Add To General Ledger	Subtract From General Ledger
a. Outstanding cheques				
b. Cheque-printing charge				
c. A collection made by the bank for the depositor				
d. A cheque written for $72.98 was recorded in the cash payments journal as $79.28				
e. A deposit in transit				
f. Bank service charges				
g. A cheque written for $543.56 was recorded in the cash payments journal as $534.56				
h. An automatic cheque for an insurance premium is included with the cancelled cheques				

NAME:

Exercise 10.8

CASH PAYMENTS JOURNAL

PAGE

Date	Cheque No.	Account Debited	Post. Ref.	Sundry Accounts Debit	Accounts Payable Debit	Purchases Debit	GST Refundable Debit	Purchases Discounts Credit	Cash Credit

NAME: ____________________

Exercise 10.9

CASH PAYMENTS JOURNAL

PAGE

Date	Cheque No.	Account Debited	Post. Ref.	Sundry Accounts Debit	Accounts Payable Debit	Purchases Debit	GST Refundable Debit	Purchases Discounts Credit	Cash Credit

NAME: ____________________

Problem 10.1

Instruction 1

Zorba's Delicatessen
Bank Reconciliation
October 31, 20XX

Bank Statement Balance	General Ledger Balance

NAME:________________________

Problem 10.1 *(continued)*

Instruction 2

GENERAL JOURNAL PAGE NO.

Date	Description	Post. Ref.	Debit	Credit

NAME: ____________________

Problem 10.2

Instruction 1

Fillie's Frocks
Bank Reconciliation
May 31, 20XX

Bank Statement Balance	General Ledger Balance

NAME:____________________

Problem 10.2 *(continued)*

Instruction 2

GENERAL JOURNAL				PAGE NO.
Date	Description	Post. Ref.	Debit	Credit

NAME: ____________________

Problem 10.3

Instruction 1

A-Z Novelties
Bank Reconciliation
January 31, 20XX

Bank Statement Balance	General Ledger Balance

NAME:____________________

Problem 10.3 *(continued)*

Instruction 2

GENERAL JOURNAL					PAGE NO.
Date		Description	Post. Ref.	Debit	Credit

NAME: ______________________

Problem 10.4

Instruction 1

Holiday Handicrafts
Bank Reconciliation
December 31, 20XX

Bank Statement Balance	General Ledger Balance

NAME:______________________

Problem 10.4 *(continued)*

Instruction 2

GENERAL JOURNAL			PAGE NO.	
Date	Description	Post. Ref.	Debit	Credit

NAME: ______________________

Problem 10.5

Instruction 1

Okanagan Valley Ski Resort
Bank Reconciliation
October 31, 20XX

Bank Statement Balance	General Ledger Balance

NAME:____________________

Problem 10.5 *(continued)*

Instruction 2

GENERAL JOURNAL PAGE NO.

Date		Description	Post. Ref.	Debit	Credit

NAME: ______________________

Problem 10.6

Instructions 1 and 4

CASH PAYMENTS JOURNAL PAGE

Date	Cheque No.	Account Debited	Post. Ref.	Sundry Accounts Debit	Accounts Payable Debit	Purchases Debit	GST Refundable Debit	Purchases Discounts Credit	Cash Credit

NAME:________________________

Problem 10.6 *(continued)*

Instructions 2, 3 and 5

PETTY CASH DISBURSEMENTS JOURNAL for MONTH of   **PAGE NO.**

Date		Voucher No.	Explanation	Receipts	Payments	Distribution of Payments				
						Postage Expense 640	Delivery Expense 620	Entertainment Expense 650	Sundry Debits	
									Acct. No.	Amount

NAME: ______________________

Problem 10.7

Instructions 1, 4 and 7

CASH PAYMENTS JOURNAL										PAGE
Date		Cheque No.	Account Debited	Post. Ref.	Sundry Accounts Debit	Accounts Payable Debit	Purchases Debit	GST Refundable Debit	Purchases Discounts Credit	Cash Credit

NAME:________________________

Problem 10.7 *(continued)*

Instructions 2, 3 and 5

PETTY CASH DISBURSEMENTS JOURNAL for MONTH of **PAGE NO.**

Date		Voucher No.	Explanation	Receipts	Payments	Distribution of Payments				
						Office Supplies 120	Postage Expense 640	Misc. Expense 670	Sundry Debits	
									Acct. No.	Amount

NAME:______________________

Problem 10.7 *(continued)*

Instructions 6 and 8

PETTY CASH DISBURSEMENTS JOURNAL for MONTH of									PAGE NO.	
						Distribution of Payments				
									Sundry Debits	
Date		Voucher No.	Explanation	Receipts	Payments	Office Supplies 120	Postage Expense 640	Misc. Expense 670	Acct. No.	Amount

NAME:____________________

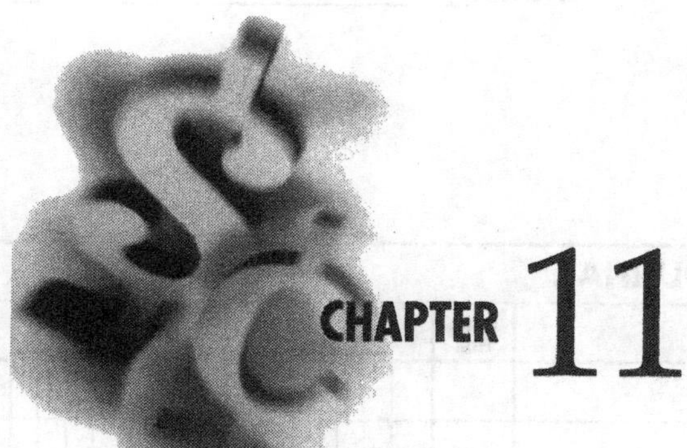

CHAPTER 11

Worksheets, Financial Statements, and Closing Entries for a Merchandising Business

Vocabulary Review

1. ____________________
2. ____________________
3. ____________________
4. ____________________
5. ____________________
6. ____________________
7. ____________________
8. ____________________
9. ____________________
10. ____________________
11. ____________________
12. ____________________

NAME:________________________

Exercise 11.1

GENERAL JOURNAL			PAGE NO.	
Date	Description	Post. Ref.	Debit	Credit

NAME: ____________________

Exercise 11.2

	Account Titles	Which section of the Balance Sheet	Normal account balance?
1.	Prepaid Insurance	____________	____________
2.	Owner's Drawing	____________	____________
3.	Accounts Payable	____________	____________
4.	Building	____________	____________
5.	Cash	____________	____________
6.	Unearned Revenue	____________	____________
7.	Accumulated Amortization	____________	____________
8.	Office Furniture	____________	____________
9.	Mortgage Payable (due in 10 years)	____________	____________
10.	Merchandise Inventory	____________	____________

	Account Titles	Which section of the Income Statement	Normal account balance?
11.	Sales Discounts	____________	____________
12.	Purchases Discounts	____________	____________
13.	Wages Expense	____________	____________
14.	Sales Returns and Allowances	____________	____________
15.	Merchandise Inventory	____________	____________
16.	Sales	____________	____________
17.	Supplies Expense	____________	____________
18.	Freight In	____________	____________
19.	Purchases	____________	____________
20.	Purchases Returns and Allowances	____________	____________

NAME:

Exercise 11.3

a.

b.

c.

d.

e.

NAME:____________________

Exercise 11.4

1. ____________________
2. ____________________
3. ____________________
4. ____________________
5. ____________________
6. ____________________
7. ____________________
8. ____________________
9. ____________________

Exercise 11.5

1.

2.

NAME:______________________________

Exercise 11.6

NAME: ______________________

Exercise 11.7

1.

2.

3. ______________________

4. ______________________

5.

NAME:______________________________

Exercise 11.8

GENERAL JOURNAL			PAGE NO.	
Date	Description	Post. Ref.	Debit	Credit

NAME:____________________

Exercise 11.8 *(continued)*

GENERAL JOURNAL			PAGE NO.	
Date	Description	Post. Ref.	Debit	Credit

NAME:______________________

Exercise 11.9

GENERAL JOURNAL			PAGE NO.	
Date	Description	Post. Ref.	Debit	Credit

NAME:________________________

Exercise 11.9 *(continued)*

GENERAL JOURNAL				PAGE NO.
Date	Description	Post. Ref.	Debit	Credit

NAME:________________________

Problem 11.1

Instruction 1

GENERAL JOURNAL			PAGE NO. 13		
Date		**Description**	**Post. Ref.**	**Debit**	**Credit**
20XX		Closing Entries			
Jan.	31	Merchandise Inventory		12100—	
		Sales		25000—	
		Purchases Returns & Allowances		480—	
		Purchases Discounts		165—	
		Income Summary			37745—
		To close Income Statement accounts with credit balances			
		and to enter the Ending Inventory on the books			
	31	Income Summary		34210—	
		Merchandise Inventory			13400—
		Sales Returns & Allowances			1400—
		Sales Discounts			900—
		Purchases			16500—
		Rent Expense			900—
		Utilities Expense			380—
		Advertising Expense			520—
		Insurance Expense			210—
		To close Income Statement accounts with debit balances			
		and to close out Beginning Merchandise Inventory			

NAME:________________________

Problem 11.1 *(continued)*

Instruction 1

Date		Description	Post. Ref.	Debit	Credit
GENERAL JOURNAL					**PAGE NO. 14**
20XX Jan.	31	Income Summary		3535—	
		Henry Higgins, Capital			3535—
		To transfer Net Income to Capital			
	31	Henry Higgins, Capital		2200—	
		Henry Higgins, Drawing			2200—
		To transfer the balance of Drawing to Capital			

NAME:________________________

Problem 11.1 *(continued)*

Instruction 1

Merchandise Inventory 130

1/31 Balance 13,400	

Henry Higgins, Capital 310

	1/31 Balance 15,200

Henry Higgins, Drawing 320

1/31 Balance 2,200	

Income Summary 330

Sales 410

	1/31 Balance 25,000

Sales Returns & Allowances 420

1/31 Balance 1,400	

Sales Discounts 430

1/31 Balance 900	

Purchases 510

1/31 Balance 16,500	

Purchases Returns & Allow. 520

	1/31 Balance 480

Purchases Discounts 530

	1/31 Balance 165

Rent Expense 610

1/31 Balance 900	

Utilities Expense 620

1/31 Balance 380	

Advertising Expense 630

1/31 Balance 520	

Insurance Expense 640

1/31 Balance 210	

NAME:________________________

Problem 11.1 *(continued)*

Instruction 2

a. ____

b. ____

c. ____

d. ____

e. ____

f. ____

NAME:________________

Problem 11.2

Instruction 1

GENERAL JOURNAL			PAGE NO.	
Date	Description	Post. Ref.	Debit	Credit

NAME:

Problem 11.2 *(continued)*

Instruction 1

GENERAL JOURNAL				PAGE NO.
Date	Description	Post. Ref.	Debit	Credit

Problem 11.2 *(continued)*

NAME: ______________________

Instruction 2

NAME:____________________

Problem 11.3

Instruction 1

____

____

____

NAME:________________________

Problem 11.3 *(continued)*

Instruction 1

NAME:________________________

Problem 11.3 *(continued)*

Instruction 2

____

____

____

____

____

Instruction 3

____

____

____

____

Problem 11.4

NAME:________________________

Instructions 1, 2, 3 and 4

Woman Source
Worksheet
For the Month Ended April 30, 20XX

Acct. No.	Account Title	Unadjusted Trial Balance Debit	Unadjusted Trial Balance Credit	Adjustments Debit	Adjustments Credit
101	Cash	10400—			
110	Accounts Receivable	3300—			
120	Notes Receivable	9600—			
130	Merchandise Inventory	31000—			
140	Supplies	760—			
150	Prepaid Insurance	2300—			
160	Office Equipment	27000—			
161	Acc. Amortization – Office Equip.		6750—		
170	Delivery Equipment	40000—			
171	Acc. Amortization – Delivery Equip.		9375—		
180	Building	35000—			
181	Acc. Amortization – Building		1500—		
210	Accounts Payable		5100—		
220	Notes Payable		40000—		
240	Unearned Revenue		1800—		
250	Mortgage Payable		30000—		
310	Gail Greenwood, Capital		67265—		
320	Gail Greenwood, Drawing	4400—			
410	Sales		60000—		
420	Sales Returns & Allowances	690—			
430	Sales Discounts	1600—			
501	Purchases	49000—			
520	Purchases Returns & Allowances		1110—		
530	Purchases Discounts		980—		
540	Freight In	2500—			
610	Rent Expense	1400—			
620	Utilities Expense	370—			
630	Wages Expense	3160—			
640	Advertising Expense	1400—			
	Totals	223880—	223880—		
650	Supplies Expense				
660	Insurance Expense				
670	Amortization Expense				
260	Wages Payable				

NAME:

Problem 11.4 *(continued)*

Instructions 1, 2, 3 and 4

Adjusted Trial Balance		Income Statement		Balance Sheet	
Debit	Credit	Debit	Credit	Debit	Credit

NAME:______________________

Problem 11.4 *(continued)*

Instructions 1, 8 and 9

GENERAL LEDGER

Cash **101**

Debit	Credit
4/30 Balance 10,400	

Accounts Receivable **110**

Debit	Credit
4/30 Balance 3,300	

Notes Receivable **120**

Debit	Credit
4/30 Balance 9,600	

Merchandise Inventory **130**

Debit	Credit
4/30 Balance 31,000	

Supplies **140**

Debit	Credit
4/30 Balance 760	

Prepaid Insurance **150**

Debit	Credit
4/30 Balance 2,300	

Office Equipment **160**

Debit	Credit
4/30 Balance 27,000	

Accumulated Amortization: Office Equip. **161**

Debit	Credit
	4/30 Balance 6,750

Delivery Equipment **170**

Debit	Credit
4/30 Balance 40,000	

Accumulated Amortization: Delivery Equip. **171**

Debit	Credit
	4/30 Balance 9,375

NAME:________________________

Problem 11.4 *(continued)*

Instructions 1, 8 and 9

Building — 180

Debit	Credit
4/30 Balance 35,000	

Accumulated Amortization: Building — 181

Debit	Credit
	4/30 Balance 1,500

Accounts Payable — 210

Debit	Credit
	4/30 Balance 5,100

Notes Payable — 220

Debit	Credit
	4/30 Balance 40,000

Unearned Revenue — 240

Debit	Credit
	4/30 Balance 1,800

Mortgage Payable — 250

Debit	Credit
	4/30 Balance 30,000

Wages Payable — 260

Debit	Credit

Gail Greenwood, Capital — 310

Debit	Credit
	4/30 Balance 67,265

Gail Greenwood, Drawing — 320

Debit	Credit
4/30 Balance 4,400	

Income Summary — 330

Debit	Credit

Sales — 410

Debit	Credit
	4/30 Balance 60,000

Sales Returns & Allowances — 420

Debit	Credit
4/30 Balance 690	

NAME:______________________

Problem 11.4 *(continued)*

Instructions 1, 8 and 9

Sales Discounts 430

Debit	Credit
4/30 Balance 1,600	

Purchases 501

Debit	Credit
4/30 Balance 49,000	

Purchases Returns & Allowances 520

Debit	Credit
	4/30 Balance 1,110

Purchases Discounts 530

Debit	Credit
	4/30 Balance 980

Freight In 540

Debit	Credit
4/30 Balance 2,500	

Rent Expense 610

Debit	Credit
4/30 Balance 1,400	

Utilities Expense 620

Debit	Credit
4/30 Balance 370	

Wages Expense 630

Debit	Credit
4/30 Balance 3,160	

Advertising Expense 640

Debit	Credit
4/30 Balance 1,400	

Supplies Expense 650

Debit	Credit

Insurance Expense 660

Debit	Credit

Amortization Expense 670

Debit	Credit

Problem 11.4 *(continued)*

NAME: ____________________

Instruction 5 ____________________

NAME:________________________

Problem 11.4 *(continued)*

Instruction 6

____

____

____

NAME: ______________________

Problem 11.4 *(continued)*

Instruction 7

NAME:______________________

Problem 11.4 *(continued)*

Instruction 7

____

____

____

NAME: ______________________________

Problem 11.4 *(continued)*

Instruction 8

GENERAL JOURNAL				PAGE NO.
Date	Description	Post. Ref.	Debit	Credit

NAME:

Problem 11.4 *(continued)*

Instruction 9

GENERAL JOURNAL			PAGE NO.	
Date	Description	Post. Ref.	Debit	Credit

NAME: ____________________

Problem 11.4 *(continued)*

Instruction 9

GENERAL JOURNAL				PAGE NO.	
Date		Description	Post. Ref.	Debit	Credit

NAME:______________________________

Problem 11.4 *(continued)*

Instruction 10

____

____

____

NAME:______________________

Problem 11.5

Instruction 1

NAME:________________________

Problem 11.5 *(continued)*

Instruction 1

NAME:______________________

Problem 11.5 *(continued)*

Instruction 2

NAME:______________________

Problem 11.5 *(continued)*

Instruction 2

____

____

____

NAME:________________________

Problem 11.5 *(continued)*

Instruction 3

GENERAL JOURNAL | **PAGE NO.**

Date		Description	Post. Ref.	Debit	Credit

NAME:________________________

Problem 11.5 *(continued)*

Instruction 3

GENERAL JOURNAL — **PAGE NO.**

Date		Description	Post. Ref.	Debit	Credit

NAME:________________________

Problem 11.5 *(continued)*

Instruction 4

Instruction 5

NAME:______________________________

Comprehensive Problem 2

Instructions 2, 9 and 10

SALES JOURNAL									PAGE
Date		Sales Invoice Number	Customer's Name	Post. Ref.	Accounts Receivable Debit	PST Payable Credit	GST Payable Credit	Sales Credit	

Instructions 3, 9 and 10

PURCHASES JOURNAL								PAGE
Date		Supplier's Name	Invoice Number	Post. Ref.	Purchases Debit	GST Refundable Debit	Accounts Payable Credit	

NAME: ____________________

Comprehensive Problem 2 *(continued)*

Instructions 5 and 10

CASH RECEIPTS JOURNAL									PAGE
Date	Received From	Account Credited	Post. Ref.	Sundry Credits	Accounts Receivable Credit	Sales Credit	PST Payable Credit	GST Payable Credit	Cash Debit

NAME: ____________________

Comprehensive Problem 2 *(continued)* Instructions 6 and 10

CASH PAYMENTS JOURNAL — PAGE

Date	Cheque No.	Account Debited	Post. Ref.	Sundry Accounts Debit	Accounts Payable Debit	Purchases Debit	GST Refundable Debit	Purchases Discounts Credit	Cash Credit

NAME: ____________________

Comprehensive Problem 2 *(continued)*

Instructions 5, 9 and 10

CASH PAYMENTS JOURNAL									PAGE
Date	Cheque No.	Account Debited	Post. Ref.	Sundry Accounts Debit	Accounts Payable Debit	Purchases Debit	GST Refundable Debit	Purchases Discounts Credit	Cash Credit

NAME:________________________

Comprehensive Problem 2 *(continued)*

Instructions 6 and 13

GENERAL JOURNAL — PAGE NO.

Date		Description	Post. Ref.	Debit	Credit

NAME: ____________________

Comprehensive Problem 2 *(continued)*

Instructions 7 and 13

GENERAL JOURNAL					PAGE NO.
Date		Description	Post. Ref.	Debit	Credit

NAME:_______________________

Comprehensive Problem 2 *(continued)*

Instructions 7 and 8

PETTY CASH DISBURSEMENTS JOURNAL for MONTH of										PAGE NO.	
						Distribution of Payments					
										Sundry Debits	
Date		Voucher No.	Explanation	Receipts	Payments	Subscription Expense 670	Postage Expense 680	Entertainment Expense 690	GST Refundable 242	Acct. No.	Amount

NAME:________________________

Comprehensive Problem 2 *(continued)*

Instructions 1, 6, 10, 13, 21/22

GENERAL LEDGER

CASH — ACCT. NO. 101

Date		Explanation	Post. Ref.	Debit	Credit	Balance
20XX Jan.	1	Balance	✓			15 399 63

PETTY CASH — ACCT. NO. 105

Date		Explanation	Post. Ref.	Debit	Credit	Balance

CHANGE FUND — ACCT. NO. 110

Date		Explanation	Post. Ref.	Debit	Credit	Balance
20XX Jan.	1	Balance	✓			300 —

ACCOUNTS RECEIVABLE — ACCT. NO. 120

Date		Explanation	Post. Ref.	Debit	Credit	Balance
20XX Jan.	1	Balance	✓			924 30

PREPAID INSURANCE — ACCT. NO. 130

Date		Explanation	Post. Ref.	Debit	Credit	Balance

NAME:______________________

Comprehensive Problem 2 *(continued)*

Instructions 1, 6, 10, 13, 21/22

OFFICE SUPPLIES — **ACCT. NO. 140**

Date		Explanation	Post. Ref.	Debit	Credit	Balance
20XX Jan.	1	Balance	✓			642 50

MERCHANDISE INVENTORY — **ACCT. NO. 145**

Date		Explanation	Post. Ref.	Debit	Credit	Balance
20XX Jan.	1	Balance	✓			17895 —

OFFICE EQUIPMENT — **ACCT. NO. 150**

Date		Explanation	Post. Ref.	Debit	Credit	Balance
20XX Jan.	1	Balance	✓			12400 —

ACCUMULATED AMORTIZATION: OFFICE EQUIPMENT — **ACCT. NO. 151**

Date		Explanation	Post. Ref.	Debit	Credit	Balance
20XX Jan.	1	Balance	✓			4800 —

STORE EQUIPMENT — **ACCT. NO. 160**

Date		Explanation	Post. Ref.	Debit	Credit	Balance
20XX Jan.	1	Balance	✓			18600 —

ACCUMULATED AMORTIZATION: STORE EQUIPMENT — **ACCT. NO. 161**

Date		Explanation	Post. Ref.	Debit	Credit	Balance
20XX Jan.	1	Balance	✓			4500 —

NAME:________________________

Comprehensive Problem 2 *(continued)*

Instructions 1, 6, 10, 13, 21/22

OFFICE FURNITURE — **ACCT. NO. 170**

Date		Explanation	Post. Ref.	Debit	Credit	Balance
20XX Jan.	1	Balance	✓			2790—

ACCUMULATED AMORTIZATION: OFFICE FURNITURE — **ACCT. NO. 171**

Date		Explanation	Post. Ref.	Debit	Credit	Balance
20XX Jan.	1	Balance	✓			1395—

VAN — **ACCT. NO. 180**

Date		Explanation	Post. Ref.	Debit	Credit	Balance
20XX Jan.	1	Balance	✓			21800—

ACCUMULATED AMORTIZATION: VAN — **ACCT. NO. 181**

Date		Explanation	Post. Ref.	Debit	Credit	Balance
20XX Jan.	1	Balance	✓			7200—

ACCOUNTS PAYABLE — **ACCT. NO. 210**

Date		Explanation	Post. Ref.	Debit	Credit	Balance
20XX Jan.	1	Balance	✓			207794

NAME: ______________________

Comprehensive Problem 2 *(continued)*

Instructions 1, 6, 10, 13, 21/22

NOTES PAYABLE — **ACCT. NO. 220**

Date		Explanation	Post. Ref.	Debit	Credit	Balance
20XX Jan.	1	Balance	✓			30620—

PROVINCIAL SALES TAX PAYABLE — **ACCT. NO. 230**

Date		Explanation	Post. Ref.	Debit	Credit	Balance
20XX Jan.	1	Balance	✓			60540

GST PAYABLE — **ACCT. NO. 240**

Date		Explanation	Post. Ref.	Debit	Credit	Balance
20XX Jan.	1	Balance	✓			52973

NAME:________________________

Comprehensive Problem 2 *(continued)*

Instructions 1, 6, 10, 13, 21/22

GST REFUNDABLE — ACCT. NO. 242

Date		Explanation	Post. Ref.	Debit	Credit	Balance
20XX Jan.	1	Balance	✓			306.25

GST OWING (REFUND) — ACCT. NO. 244

Date		Explanation	Post. Ref.	Debit	Credit	Balance

HOLLY HARRIS, CAPITAL — ACCT. NO. 301

Date		Explanation	Post. Ref.	Debit	Credit	Balance
20XX Jan.	1	Balance	✓			39329.61

HOLLY HARRIS, DRAWING — ACCT. NO. 310

Date		Explanation	Post. Ref.	Debit	Credit	Balance

INCOME SUMMARY — ACCT. NO. 320

Date		Explanation	Post. Ref.	Debit	Credit	Balance

NAME:________________________

Comprehensive Problem 2 *(continued)*

Instructions 1, 6, 10, 13, 21/22

REVENUE FROM SALES **ACCT. NO. 410**

Date		Explanation	Post. Ref.	Debit	Credit	Balance

SALES RETURNS AND ALLOWANCES **ACCT. NO. 420**

Date		Explanation	Post. Ref.	Debit	Credit	Balance

PURCHASES **ACCT. NO. 510**

Date		Explanation	Post. Ref.	Debit	Credit	Balance

PURCHASES RETURNS AND ALLOWANCES **ACCT. NO. 520**

Date		Explanation	Post. Ref.	Debit	Credit	Balance

PURCHASES DISCOUNTS **ACCT. NO. 530**

Date		Explanation	Post. Ref.	Debit	Credit	Balance

FREIGHT IN **ACCT. NO. 540**

Date		Explanation	Post. Ref.	Debit	Credit	Balance

NAME:______________________________

Comprehensive Problem 2 *(continued)*

Instructions 1, 6, 10, 13, 21/22

RENT EXPENSE — **ACCT. NO. 610**

Date		Explanation	Post. Ref.	Debit	Credit	Balance

UTILITIES EXPENSE — **ACCT. NO. 620**

Date		Explanation	Post. Ref.	Debit	Credit	Balance

OFFICE SUPPLIES EXPENSE — **ACCT. NO. 625**

Date		Explanation	Post. Ref.	Debit	Credit	Balance

INTEREST EXPENSE — **ACCT. NO. 630**

Date		Explanation	Post. Ref.	Debit	Credit	Balance

INSURANCE EXPENSE — **ACCT. NO. 635**

Date		Explanation	Post. Ref.	Debit	Credit	Balance

WAGES EXPENSE — **ACCT. NO. 640**

Date		Explanation	Post. Ref.	Debit	Credit	Balance

NAME: ____________________

Comprehensive Problem 2 *(continued)*

Instructions 1, 6, 10, 13, 21/22

ADVERTISING EXPENSE

ACCT. NO. 650

Date		Explanation	Post. Ref.	Debit	Credit	Balance

AMORTIZATION EXPENSE

ACCT. NO. 655

Date		Explanation	Post. Ref.	Debit	Credit	Balance

DELIVERY EXPENSE

ACCT. NO. 660

Date		Explanation	Post. Ref.	Debit	Credit	Balance

SUBSCRIPTION EXPENSE

ACCT. NO. 670

Date		Explanation	Post. Ref.	Debit	Credit	Balance

POSTAGE EXPENSE

ACCT. NO. 680

Date		Explanation	Post. Ref.	Debit	Credit	Balance

ENTERTAINMENT EXPENSE

ACCT. NO. 690

Date		Explanation	Post. Ref.	Debit	Credit	Balance

NAME:______________________

Comprehensive Problem 2 *(continued)*

Instructions 1, 6, 10, 13, 21/22

BANK CHARGES EXPENSE — ACCT. NO. 695

Date		Explanation	Post. Ref.	Debit	Credit	Balance

Instructions 1, 6, 10/13

ACCOUNTS RECEIVABLE SUBSIDIARY LEDGER

CULVER, DAVE

Date		Explanation	Post. Ref.	Debit	Credit	Balance
20XX Jan.	1	Balance	✓			2 7 5 15

GOODE, JILL

Date		Explanation	Post. Ref.	Debit	Credit	Balance
20XX Jan.	1	Balance	✓			2 9 1 05

MORRISON, LYNDA

Date		Explanation	Post. Ref.	Debit	Credit	Balance
20XX Jan.	1	Balance	✓			1 4 3 50

NAME: ______________________

Comprehensive Problem 2 *(continued)*

Instructions 1, 6, 10/13

VERMONT, PETER

Date		Explanation	Post. Ref.	Debit	Credit	Balance
20XX Jan.	1	Balance	✓			2 1 4 60

ACCOUNTS PAYABLE SUBSIDIARY LEDGER

ADULT TOYS

Date		Explanation	Post. Ref.	Debit	Credit	Balance
20XX Jan.	1	Balance	✓			9 0 0 94

MODEL SUPPLIES

Date		Explanation	Post. Ref.	Debit	Credit	Balance
20XX Jan.	1	Balance	✓			7 1 4 76

THE TOY PLACE

Date		Explanation	Post. Ref.	Debit	Credit	Balance
20XX Jan.	1	Balance	✓			4 6 2 24

NAME: ____________________

Comprehensive Problem 2 *(continued)*

Instruction 12

____

____

____

Bank Statement Balance	General Ledger Balance
Add:	Add:
Deduct:	Deduct:

NAME: ______________________________

Comprehensive Problem 2 *(continued)*

Instruction 17

NAME:________________________

Comprehensive Problem 2 *(continued)*

Instructions 14, 15 and 16

Hobby House					
Worksheet					
For Month Ended January 31, 20XX					
Acct. No.	**Account Titles**	**Unadjusted Trial Balance**		**Adjustments**	
		Debit	**Credit**	**Debit**	**Credit**
101	Cash	20232 67			
105	Petty Cash	100 —			
110	Change Fund	300 —			
120	Accounts Receivable	585 40			
130	Prepaid Insurance	360 —			
140	Office Supplies	673 40			
145	Merchandise Inventory	17895 —			
150	Office Equipment	23100 —			
151	Acc. Amortization — Office Equip.		4800 —		
160	Store Equipment	18600 —			
161	Acc. Amortization — Store Equip.		4500 —		
170	Office Furniture	2790 —			
171	Acc. Amortization — Office Furn.		1395 —		
180	Van	21800 —			
181	Acc. Amortization — Van		7200 —		
210	Accounts Payable		2805 54		
220	Notes Payable		41558 —		
230	PST Payable		1344 56		
301	Holly Harris, Capital		39329 61		
310	Holly Harris, Drawing	1600 —			
410	Revenue from Sales		16837 —		
420	Sales Returns & Allowances	30 —			
510	Purchases	7890 —			

NAME: ______________________

Adjusted Trial Balance		Income Statement		Balance Sheet	
Debit	Credit	Debit	Credit	Debit	Credit

NAME:____________________

Comprehensive Problem 2 *(continued)*

Instructions 14, 15 and 16

Hobby House						
Worksheet						
For Month Ended January 31, 20XX						
Acct. No.	Account Titles	Unadjusted Trial Balance		Adjustments		
		Debit	Credit	Debit	Credit	
520	Purchases Ret. & Allow.		120 —			
530	Purchases Discount		66 76			
540	Freight In	100 —				
610	Rent Expense	1400 —				
620	Utilities Expense	275 60				
625	Office Supplies Expense					
630	Interest Expense	459 —				
635	Insurance Expense					
640	Wages Expense	1475 —				
650	Advertising Expense	150 —				
655	Amortization Expense					
660	Delivery Expense	8 45				
670	Subscription Expense	36 45				
680	Postage Expense	8 30				
690	Entertainment Expense	36 20				
695	Bank Expense Charges	51 —				
	Totals	119956 47	119956 47			

NAME:______________________________

Adjusted Trial Balance		Income Statement		Balance Sheet	
Debit	Credit	Debit	Credit	Debit	Credit

NAME:________________________

Comprehensive Problem 2 *(continued)*

Instruction 18

____

____

____

NAME:____________________

Comprehensive Problem 2 *(continued)*

Instruction 18

Instruction 19

NAME:____________________

Comprehensive Problem 2 *(continued)*

Instruction 20

NAME:________________________

Comprehensive Problem 2 *(continued)*

Instruction 20

NAME:________________________

Comprehensive Problem 2 *(continued)*

Instructions 21 and 22

GENERAL JOURNAL				PAGE NO.
Date	Description	Post. Ref.	Debit	Credit

NAME:______________________

Comprehensive Problem 2 *(continued)*

Instructions 21 and 22

GENERAL JOURNAL			PAGE NO.	
Date	Description	Post. Ref.	Debit	Credit

NAME:______________________________

Comprehensive Problem 2 *(continued)*

Instructions 21 and 22

GENERAL JOURNAL				PAGE NO.	
Date		Description	Post. Ref.	Debit	Credit

NAME:______________________

Comprehensive Problem 2 *(continued)*

Instruction 23

____

____

____

NAME: ______________________

CHAPTER 12

Payroll—Employee Deductions

Vocabulary Review

1. ______________________
2. ______________________
3. ______________________
4. ______________________
5. ______________________
6. ______________________
7. ______________________
8. ______________________
9. ______________________
10. ______________________
11. ______________________
12. ______________________
13. ______________________
14. ______________________
15. ______________________
16. ______________________
17. ______________________
18. ______________________
19. ______________________
20. ______________________
21. ______________________
22. ______________________
23. ______________________
24. ______________________
25. ______________________
26. ______________________
27. ______________________
28. ______________________
29. ______________________
30. ______________________
31. ______________________
32. ______________________
33. ______________________
34. ______________________

NAME:______________________

Exercise 12.1

Employee	Hours Worked	Hourly Wage	Regular Earnings	Overtime Earnings	Gross Earnings
Goldstein	48	$10.50			
McDonald	50	8.60			
Murray	42	9.60			
Huang	46	8.80			
Totals					

Exercise 12.2

Employee	Gross Pay	CPP Contribution	EI Premium
McGregor	$559.99		
Mandela	602.70		
Goodman	665.12		
Chang	562.00		
Chavez	642.60		
Bartz	669.55		
Totals			

NAME:____________________

Exercise 12.3

Employee	Total Exemptions	Federal Claim Code	Provincial Claim Code
Mandrake	$ 7,400.00		
Graham	7,425.00		
Williams	17,200.00		
Deschutes	12,200.00		
Cropier	9,030.00		

Exercise 12.4

Exercise 12.5

Employee	Hours Worked M	Tu	W	Th	Hourly Wage	Regular Earnings	Overtime Earnings	Gross Earnings
Habib	10	10	12	8	$14.20			
Wiggins	10	10	14	10	12.80			
Montoya	12	12	12	12	10.66			
Nanook	14	12	10	10	12.44			
Totals								

NAME:________________________

Exercise 12.6

Employee	Federal Claim Code	Provincial Claim Code	Earnings	Federal Income Tax	Provincial Income Tax
Samaan	1	1	$ 901.00	______	______
Thomson	3	3	1,217.00	______	______
Culver	2	3	1,557.00	______	______
Santana	4	5	685.00	______	______
Chow	6	6	641.00	______	______
Totals			______	______	______

Exercise 12.7

Regular earnings	$1,269.38
Overtime earnings	a. __________
Gross earnings	$1,737.70
CPP contributions	31.74
EI premiums	b. __________
Federal income tax withheld	301.69
Provincial income tax withheld	50.45
Charitable contributions withheld	89.00
Savings withheld	18.00
Total deductions	c. __________
Net earnings	$1,204.55

NAME:________________________

Exercise 12.8

GENERAL JOURNAL				PAGE NO.	
Date		Description	Post. Ref.	Debit	Credit

NAME:______________________

Problem 12.1

Employee	Hours Worked	Salary or Hourly Wage	(a) Regular Earnings	(b) Overtime Earnings	(c) Gross Earnings
Suter	50	$49,140/yr.			
Heintz	48	48,100/yr.			
Wong	46	12.50/hr.			
Bracken	50	9.20/hr.			
Chicos	60	7.76/hr.			
Totals					

NAME: ____________________

Problem 12.2

Instruction 1

PAYROLL REGISTER — Week of ____________ 20XX

Employee	Total Hours	Hourly Rate	Regular Earnings	Overtime Earnings	Gross Earnings	Fed'l Claim Code	Prov'l Claim Code	Deductions: CPP Contributions	EI Premiums	Fed'l Income Tax	Prov'l Income Tax	Charitable Contributions	Total Deductions	Net Earnings
O'Shaunessy	40	$15.02				4	5							
LeMonde	44	13.20				1	1							
Johnstone	48	14.60				3	3							
Kelly	40	16.80				5	5							
Laurent	45	15.02				2	3							
Totals														

NAME:____________________

Problem 12.2 *(continued)*

Instruction 2

GENERAL JOURNAL			PAGE NO.	
Date	Description	Post. Ref.	Debit	Credit

NAME: ____________________

Problem 12.3

Instruction 1

PAYROLL REGISTER								Week of ______ 20XX						
								Deductions						
Employee	Total Hours	Hourly Rate	Regular Earnings	Overtime Earnings	Gross Earnings	Fed'l Claim Code	Prov'l Claim Code	CPP Contributions	EI Premiums	Fed'l Income Tax	Prov'l Income Tax	Charitable Contributions	Total Deductions	Net Earnings
Corbeil	45	$13.80												
Bergeron	46	14.20												
Wellington	45	14.20												
DaVinci	36	16.40												
MacKay	44	15.40												
Weaver	40	18.00												
Totals														

NAME:____________________

Problem 12.3 *(continued)*

Instruction 2

GENERAL JOURNAL			PAGE NO.	
Date	Description	Post. Ref.	Debit	Credit

NAME: ______________________

Problem 12.4

Instruction 1

PAYROLL REGISTER Week of __________ 20XX

Employee	Total Hours	Hourly Rate	Regular Earnings	Overtime Earnings	Gross Earnings	Fed'l Claim Code	Prov'l Claim Code	Deductions: CPP Contributions	EI Premiums	Fed'l Income Tax	Prov'l Income Tax	Employee Savings	Total Deductions	Net Earnings
McIntosh	Mgmt.	—												
Dinh	Mgmt.	—												
Duclos	38	$14.20												
Martini	45	14.20												
Ifrah	44	14.80												
St. James	40	14.80												
Totals														

NAME:______________________

Problem 12.4 *(continued)*

Instruction 2

GENERAL JOURNAL			PAGE NO.	
Date	Description	Post. Ref.	Debit	Credit

NAME:______________________

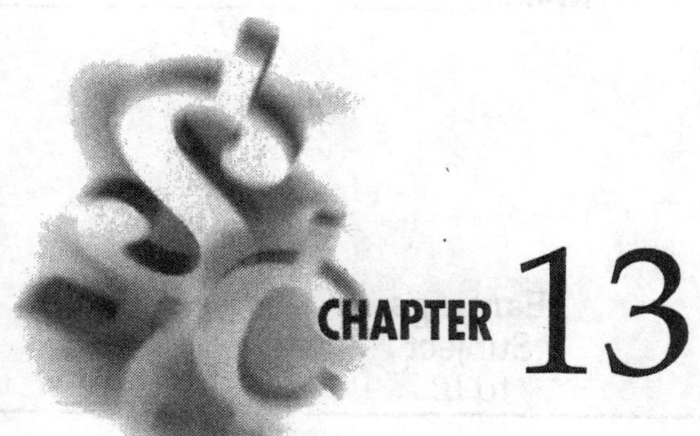

CHAPTER 13

Payroll—Employer Taxes and Other Obligations

Vocabulary Review

1. ______________________
2. ______________________
3. ______________________
4. ______________________
5. ______________________
6. ______________________
7. ______________________
8. ______________________
9. ______________________
10. ______________________
11. ______________________
12. ______________________

NAME:________________________

Exercise 13.1

a-b.

Employee	Earnings Subject to CPP	CPP Contribution	Earnings Subject to EI	EI Premium
1.				
2.				
3.				
4.				
5.				
6.				
Totals				

c. Employer's Wages Expense

____

____

d. Employer's Payroll Tax Expense

____

____

____

NAME:________________________

Exercise 13.2

GENERAL JOURNAL **PAGE NO.**

Date		Description	Post. Ref.	Debit	Credit

NAME:______________________

Exercise 13.3

a.

GENERAL JOURNAL					PAGE NO.
Date		Description	Post. Ref.	Debit	Credit

b. ____

____

____

____

NAME:________________________________

Exercise 13.4

GENERAL JOURNAL				PAGE NO.	
Date		Description	Post. Ref.	Debit	Credit

NAME:________________________

Exercise 13.5

a.

GENERAL JOURNAL				PAGE NO.	
Date		Description	Post. Ref.	Debit	Credit

b.

GENERAL JOURNAL				PAGE NO.	
Date		Description	Post. Ref.	Debit	Credit

NAME:______________________

Exercise 13.6

a-b.

Employee	Weekly Pay	Cumulative Through November	Dec. 1–7 Taxable Wages for CPP	CPP Contribution	Dec. 1–7 Taxable Wages for EI	EI Premium
A	$910.00	$43,680	______	—	______	______
B	700.00	38,000	______	10.01	______	______
C	800.00	38,800	______	—	______	______
D	675.00	32,400	______	26.13	______	______
E	760.00	37,900	______	14.31	______	______
	Totals		______	______	______	______

Exercise 13.7

Employer's name – Nom de l'employeur

Canada Customs and Revenue Agency / Agence des douanes et du revenu du Canada

T4

Year / Année

STATEMENT OF REMUNERATION PAID
ÉTAT DE LA RÉMUNÉRATION PAYÉE

VOID / ANNULÉ

14 Employment income – line 101 / Revenus d'emploi – ligne 101

22 Income tax deducted – line 437 / Impôt sur le revenu retenu – ligne 437

54 Business Number / Numéro d'entreprise

10 Province of employment / Province d'emploi

16 Employee's CPP contributions – line 308 / Cotisations de l'employé au RPC – ligne 308

24 EI insurable earnings / Gains assurables d'AE

12 Social insurance number / Numéro d'assurance sociale

28 Exempt – Exemption: CPP - QPP / RPC - RRQ; EI / AE

29 Employment Code / Code d'emploi

17 Employee's QPP contributions – line 308 / Cotisations de l'employé au RRQ – ligne 308

26 CPP-QPP pensionable earnings / Gains donnant droit à pension - RPC-RRQ

Employee's name and address – Nom et adresse de l'employé

Last name (in capital letters) – Nom de famille (en lettres majuscules) | First name – Prénom | Initials – Initiales

18 Employee's EI premiums – line 312 / Cotisations de l'employé à l'AE – ligne 312

44 Union dues – line 212 / Cotisations syndicales – ligne 212

20 RPP contributions – line 207 / Cotisations à un RPA – ligne 207

46 Charitable donations – Schedule 1 / Dons de bienfaisance – Annexe 1

52 Pension adjustment – line 206 / Facteur d'équivalence – ligne 206

50 RPP or DPSP registration number / N° d'agrément d'un RPA ou d'un RPDB

Other information (see the back) / Autres renseignements (voir au verso)

Box – Case | Amount – Montant | Box – Case | Amount – Montant

Box – Case | Amount – Montant | Box – Case | Amount – Montant | Box – Case | Amount – Montant | Box – Case | Amount – Montant

T4 (01)

NAME:____________________

Problem 13.1

EMPLOYEE'S INDIVIDUAL EARNINGS RECORD

Name: __________ Employee No.: __________ Date Employed: __________

Address: __________ Social Insurance No.: __________

Female: _____ Male: _____ Federal Net Claim Code: _____

Married: _____ Single: _____ Provincial Net Claim Code: _____

Phone No.: __________ Date of Birth: __________ Pay Rate: __________ Per: _____

Period Ending	Gross Earnings	Deductions						Net Pay	Cheque No.
		CPP Contributions	EI Premiums	Federal Income Tax	Provincial Income Tax	Union Dues	Total Deductions		
Cumulative to Dec. 1									

NAME:_________________________

Problem 13.2 *(continued)*

Instruction 1

GENERAL LEDGER

CASH **ACCT. NO. 110**

Date		Explanation	Post. Ref.	Debit	Credit	Balance
20XX June	1	Balance Forward	✓			17900—

CANADA PENSION PLAN PAYABLE **ACCT. NO. 210**

Date		Explanation	Post. Ref.	Debit	Credit	Balance
20XX June	1	Balance Forward	✓			73616

NAME:________________________

Problem 13.2 *(continued)*

Instructions 1 and 2

EMPLOYMENT INSURANCE PAYABLE — **ACCT. NO. 215**

Date		Explanation	Post. Ref.	Debit	Credit	Balance
20XX June	1	Balance Forward	✓			4 6 2 24

FEDERAL INCOME TAX PAYABLE — **ACCT. NO. 220**

Date		Explanation	Post. Ref.	Debit	Credit	Balance
19XX June	1	Balance Forward	✓			1 8 7 4 40

PROVINCIAL INCOME TAX PAYABLE — **ACCT. NO. 225**

Date		Explanation	Post. Ref.	Debit	Credit	Balance
20XX June	1	Balance Forward	✓			4 6 2 25

WAGES PAYABLE — **ACCT. NO. 240**

Date		Explanation	Post. Ref.	Debit	Credit	Balance

NAME:____________________

Problem 13.2 *(continued)*

Instructions 1 and 2

WAGES EXPENSE — **ACCT. NO. 610**

Date		Explanation	Post. Ref.	Debit	Credit	Balance

PAYROLL TAX EXPENSE — **ACCT. NO. 620**

Date		Explanation	Post. Ref.	Debit	Credit	Balance

NAME:________________________

Problem 13.2 *(continued)*

Instruction 2

GENERAL JOURNAL				PAGE NO.	
Date		Description	Post. Ref.	Debit	Credit

NAME:________________________

Problem 13.2 *(continued)*

Instruction 2

GENERAL JOURNAL				PAGE NO.
Date	Description	Post. Ref.	Debit	Credit

NAME:________________________

Problem 13.2 *(continued)*

Instruction 3

a. ____

b. ____

NAME:______________________

Problem 13.3

Instruction 1

	Employee Deductions	Employer's Payroll Taxes	Total Payable
CPP			
EI			
Federal Income Tax			
Provincial Income Tax			
Totals			

Instruction 2

Canada Customs and Revenue Agency | Agence des douanes et du revenu du Canada

CURRENT SOURCE DEDUCTIONS REMITTANCE VOUCHER

002022

RC107 E (01)

YOU MUST COMPLETE THIS AREA

Business Number

Legal Name

Address

City | Province | Postal Code

Do not use this area

6

Gross payroll in remitting period (dollars only) 0 0

Number of employees in last pay period

End of remitting period for which deductions were withheld | Year | Month

Amount paid

002022 0006 0000 00 000000000000000 000000 0000000000000 7

⑆12204⑈117⑆ 96

NAME:________________________

Problem 13.3

Instruction 3

GENERAL JOURNAL					PAGE NO.
Date		Description	Post. Ref.	Debit	Credit

NAME:____________________________

Problem 13.4

Instruction 1

GENERAL JOURNAL				PAGE NO.	
Date		Description	Post. Ref.	Debit	Credit

Instruction 2

GENERAL JOURNAL				PAGE NO.	
Date		Description	Post. Ref.	Debit	Credit

NAME:________________________

Problem 13.5 Instruction 1

Employer's name – Nom de l'employeur

Canada Customs and Revenue Agency | Agence des douanes et du revenu du Canada

Year / Année

T4

STATEMENT OF REMUNERATION PAID
ÉTAT DE LA RÉMUNÉRATION PAYÉE

VOID / ANNULÉ

Employment income – line 101 / Revenus d'emploi – ligne 101 — 14

Income tax deducted – line 437 / Impôt sur le revenu retenu – ligne 437 — 22

Business Number / Numéro d'entreprise — 54

Province of employment / Province d'emploi — 10

Employee's CPP contributions – line 308 / Cotisations de l'employé au RPC – ligne 308 — 16

EI insurable earnings / Gains assurables d'AE — 24

Social insurance number / Numéro d'assurance sociale — 12

Exempt – Exemption: CPP - QPP / RPC - RRQ — 28; EI / AE

Employment Code / Code d'emploi — 29

Employee's QPP contributions – line 308 / Cotisations de l'employé au RRQ – ligne 308 — 17

CPP-QPP pensionable earnings / Gains donnant droit à pension - RPC-RRQ — 26

Employee's name and address – Nom et adresse de l'employé

Last name (in capital letters) – Nom de famille (en lettres majuscules) | First name – Prénom | Initials – Initiales

Employee's EI premiums – line 312 / Cotisations de l'employé à l'AE – ligne 312 — 18

Union dues – line 212 / Cotisations syndicales – ligne 212 — 44

RPP contributions – line 207 / Cotisations à un RPA – ligne 207 — 20

Charitable donations – Schedule 1 / Dons de bienfaisance – Annexe 1 — 46

Pension adjustment – line 206 / Facteur d'équivalence – ligne 206 — 52

RPP or DPSP registration number / N° d'agrément d'un RPA ou d'un RPDB — 50

Other information (see the back) / Autres renseignements (voir au verso)

Box – Case | Amount – Montant | Box – Case | Amount – Montant

Box – Case | Amount – Montant | Box – Case | Amount – Montant | Box – Case | Amount – Montant | Box – Case | Amount – Montant

T4 (01)

Employer's name – Nom de l'employeur

Canada Customs and Revenue Agency | Agence des douanes et du revenu du Canada

Year / Année

T4

STATEMENT OF REMUNERATION PAID
ÉTAT DE LA RÉMUNÉRATION PAYÉE

VOID / ANNULÉ

Employment income – line 101 / Revenus d'emploi – ligne 101 — 14

Income tax deducted – line 437 / Impôt sur le revenu retenu – ligne 437 — 22

Business Number / Numéro d'entreprise — 54

Province of employment / Province d'emploi — 10

Employee's CPP contributions – line 308 / Cotisations de l'employé au RPC – ligne 308 — 16

EI insurable earnings / Gains assurables d'AE — 24

Social insurance number / Numéro d'assurance sociale — 12

Exempt – Exemption: CPP - QPP / RPC - RRQ — 28; EI / AE

Employment Code / Code d'emploi — 29

Employee's QPP contributions – line 308 / Cotisations de l'employé au RRQ – ligne 308 — 17

CPP-QPP pensionable earnings / Gains donnant droit à pension - RPC-RRQ — 26

Employee's name and address – Nom et adresse de l'employé

Last name (in capital letters) – Nom de famille (en lettres majuscules) | First name – Prénom | Initials – Initiales

Employee's EI premiums – line 312 / Cotisations de l'employé à l'AE – ligne 312 — 18

Union dues – line 212 / Cotisations syndicales – ligne 212 — 44

RPP contributions – line 207 / Cotisations à un RPA – ligne 207 — 20

Charitable donations – Schedule 1 / Dons de bienfaisance – Annexe 1 — 46

Pension adjustment – line 206 / Facteur d'équivalence – ligne 206 — 52

RPP or DPSP registration number / N° d'agrément d'un RPA ou d'un RPDB — 50

Other information (see the back) / Autres renseignements (voir au verso)

Box – Case | Amount – Montant | Box – Case | Amount – Montant

Box – Case | Amount – Montant | Box – Case | Amount – Montant | Box – Case | Amount – Montant | Box – Case | Amount – Montant

T4 (01)

NAME:______________________

Problem 13.5 *(continued)* Instruction 1

Employer's name – Nom de l'employeur

Canada Customs and Revenue Agency / Agence des douanes et du revenu du Canada

Year / Année

T4

STATEMENT OF REMUNERATION PAID
ÉTAT DE LA RÉMUNÉRATION PAYÉE

VOID / ANNULÉ

14 Employment income – line 101 / Revenus d'emploi – ligne 101

22 Income tax deducted – line 437 / Impôt sur le revenu retenu – ligne 437

54 Business Number / Numéro d'entreprise

10 Province of employment / Province d'emploi

16 Employee's CPP contributions – line 308 / Cotisations de l'employé au RPC – ligne 308

24 EI insurable earnings / Gains assurables d'AE

12 Social insurance number / Numéro d'assurance sociale

Exempt – Exemption: 28 CPP - QPP / RPC - RRQ; EI / AE

29 Employment Code / Code d'emploi

17 Employee's QPP contributions – line 308 / Cotisations de l'employé au RRQ – ligne 308

26 CPP-QPP pensionable earnings / Gains donnant droit à pension - RPC-RRQ

Employee's name and address – Nom et adresse de l'employé

Last name (in capital letters) – Nom de famille (en lettres majuscules) | First name – Prénom | Initials – Initiales

18 Employee's EI premiums – line 312 / Cotisations de l'employé à l'AE – ligne 312

44 Union dues – line 212 / Cotisations syndicales – ligne 212

20 RPP contributions – line 207 / Cotisations à un RPA – ligne 207

46 Charitable donations – Schedule 1 / Dons de bienfaisance – Annexe 1

52 Pension adjustment – line 206 / Facteur d'équivalence – ligne 206

50 RPP or DPSP registration number / N° d'agrément d'un RPA ou d'un RPDB

Other information (see the back) / Autres renseignements (voir au verso)

Box – Case | Amount – Montant | Box – Case | Amount – Montant

Box – Case | Amount – Montant | Box – Case | Amount – Montant | Box – Case | Amount – Montant | Box – Case | Amount – Montant

T4 (01)

Employer's name – Nom de l'employeur

Canada Customs and Revenue Agency / Agence des douanes et du revenu du Canada

Year / Année

T4

STATEMENT OF REMUNERATION PAID
ÉTAT DE LA RÉMUNÉRATION PAYÉE

VOID / ANNULÉ

14 Employment income – line 101 / Revenus d'emploi – ligne 101

22 Income tax deducted – line 437 / Impôt sur le revenu retenu – ligne 437

54 Business Number / Numéro d'entreprise

10 Province of employment / Province d'emploi

16 Employee's CPP contributions – line 308 / Cotisations de l'employé au RPC – ligne 308

24 EI insurable earnings / Gains assurables d'AE

12 Social insurance number / Numéro d'assurance sociale

Exempt – Exemption: 28 CPP - QPP / RPC - RRQ; EI / AE

29 Employment Code / Code d'emploi

17 Employee's QPP contributions – line 308 / Cotisations de l'employé au RRQ – ligne 308

26 CPP-QPP pensionable earnings / Gains donnant droit à pension - RPC-RRQ

Employee's name and address – Nom et adresse de l'employé

Last name (in capital letters) – Nom de famille (en lettres majuscules) | First name – Prénom | Initials – Initiales

18 Employee's EI premiums – line 312 / Cotisations de l'employé à l'AE – ligne 312

44 Union dues – line 212 / Cotisations syndicales – ligne 212

20 RPP contributions – line 207 / Cotisations à un RPA – ligne 207

46 Charitable donations – Schedule 1 / Dons de bienfaisance – Annexe 1

52 Pension adjustment – line 206 / Facteur d'équivalence – ligne 206

50 RPP or DPSP registration number / N° d'agrément d'un RPA ou d'un RPDB

Other information (see the back) / Autres renseignements (voir au verso)

Box – Case | Amount – Montant | Box – Case | Amount – Montant

Box – Case | Amount – Montant | Box – Case | Amount – Montant | Box – Case | Amount – Montant | Box – Case | Amount – Montant

T4 (01)

NAME:______________________

Problem 13.5 *(continued)* Instruction 1

Employer's name – Nom de l'employeur

Canada Customs and Revenue Agency / Agence des douanes et du revenu du Canada

T4

Year / Année

STATEMENT OF REMUNERATION PAID
ÉTAT DE LA RÉMUNÉRATION PAYÉE

VOID / ANNULÉ

14 Employment income – line 101 / Revenus d'emploi – ligne 101

22 Income tax deducted – line 437 / Impôt sur le revenu retenu – ligne 437

54 Business Number / Numéro d'entreprise

10 Province of employment / Province d'emploi

16 Employee's CPP contributions – line 308 / Cotisations de l'employé au RPC – ligne 308

24 EI insurable earnings / Gains assurables d'AE

12 Social insurance number / Numéro d'assurance sociale

Exempt – Exemption: 28 CPP - QPP / RPC - RRQ; EI / AE

29 Employment Code / Code d'emploi

17 Employee's QPP contributions – line 308 / Cotisations de l'employé au RRQ – ligne 308

26 CPP-QPP pensionable earnings / Gains donnant droit à pension - RPC-RRQ

Employee's name and address – Nom et adresse de l'employé

Last name (in capital letters) – Nom de famille (en lettres majuscules) | First name – Prénom | Initials – Initiales

18 Employee's EI premiums – line 312 / Cotisations de l'employé à l'AE – ligne 312

44 Union dues – line 212 / Cotisations syndicales – ligne 212

20 RPP contributions – line 207 / Cotisations à un RPA – ligne 207

46 Charitable donations – Schedule 1 / Dons de bienfaisance – Annexe 1

52 Pension adjustment – line 206 / Facteur d'équivalence – ligne 206

50 RPP or DPSP registration number / N° d'agrément d'un RPA ou d'un RPDB

Other information (see the back) / Autres renseignements (voir au verso)

Box – Case | Amount – Montant | Box – Case | Amount – Montant

Box – Case | Amount – Montant | Box – Case | Amount – Montant | Box – Case | Amount – Montant | Box – Case | Amount – Montant

T4 (01)

Employer's name – Nom de l'employeur

Canada Customs and Revenue Agency / Agence des douanes et du revenu du Canada

T4

Year / Année

STATEMENT OF REMUNERATION PAID
ÉTAT DE LA RÉMUNÉRATION PAYÉE

VOID / ANNULÉ

14 Employment income – line 101 / Revenus d'emploi – ligne 101

22 Income tax deducted – line 437 / Impôt sur le revenu retenu – ligne 437

54 Business Number / Numéro d'entreprise

10 Province of employment / Province d'emploi

16 Employee's CPP contributions – line 308 / Cotisations de l'employé au RPC – ligne 308

24 EI insurable earnings / Gains assurables d'AE

12 Social insurance number / Numéro d'assurance sociale

Exempt – Exemption: 28 CPP - QPP / RPC - RRQ; EI / AE

29 Employment Code / Code d'emploi

17 Employee's QPP contributions – line 308 / Cotisations de l'employé au RRQ – ligne 308

26 CPP-QPP pensionable earnings / Gains donnant droit à pension - RPC-RRQ

Employee's name and address – Nom et adresse de l'employé

Last name (in capital letters) – Nom de famille (en lettres majuscules) | First name – Prénom | Initials – Initiales

18 Employee's EI premiums – line 312 / Cotisations de l'employé à l'AE – ligne 312

44 Union dues – line 212 / Cotisations syndicales – ligne 212

20 RPP contributions – line 207 / Cotisations à un RPA – ligne 207

46 Charitable donations – Schedule 1 / Dons de bienfaisance – Annexe 1

52 Pension adjustment – line 206 / Facteur d'équivalence – ligne 206

50 RPP or DPSP registration number / N° d'agrément d'un RPA ou d'un RPDB

Other information (see the back) / Autres renseignements (voir au verso)

Box – Case | Amount – Montant | Box – Case | Amount – Montant

Box – Case | Amount – Montant | Box – Case | Amount – Montant | Box – Case | Amount – Montant | Box – Case | Amount – Montant

T4 (01)

NAME:________________________

Problem 13.5 *(continued)*

Instruction 2

Canada Customs and Revenue Agency / Agence des douanes et du revenu du Canada

For the year ending December 31, / Pour l'année se terminant le 31 décembre 20____

Web Access Code – Code d'accès au Web

0505 **T4** Summary / Sommaire

SUMMARY OF REMUNERATION PAID
SOMMAIRE DE LA RÉMUNÉRATION PAYÉE

You have to file your T4 return on or before the last day of **February**.
See the information on the back of this form.

Vous devez produire votre déclaration T4 au plus tard le dernier jour de **février**.
Lisez les renseignements au verso de ce formulaire.

Business Number – Numéro d'entreprise

Name and address of employer – Nom et adresse de l'employeur

Total number of T4 slips filed – Nombre total de feuillets T4 produits
88

Employment income – Revenus d'emploi
14

Registered pension plan (RPP) contributions
Cotisations à un régime de pension agréé (RPA)
20

Pension adjustment – Facteur d'équivalence
52

Indicate how many T4 slips are for employees whose addresses are in the U.S.A.

Indiquez le nombre de feuillets T4 émis pour des employés dont l'adresse est aux États-Unis.

Employee's CPP contributions – Cotisations de l'employé au RPC
16

Employer's CPP contributions – Cotisations de l'employeur au RPC
27

Employee's EI premiums – Cotisations de l'employé à l'AE
18

Employer's EI premiums – Cotisations de l'employeur à l'AE
19

Income tax deducted – Impôt sur le revenu retenu
22

Total deductions reported (16 + 27 + 18 + 19 + 22)
Total des retenues déclarées (16 + 27 + 18 + 19 + 22)
80

Minus: remittances – Moins : versements
82

We do not charge or refund a difference of less than $2.

Nous n'exigeons ni ne remboursons une différence inférieure à 2 $.

Difference – Différence

Do not use this area – N'inscrivez rien ici

90 Last to current / Précédente à courante 1 2 Other / Autre 3

91 Pro Forma 1 2

93 Y – A D – J

94 PD15-1

96 POF PSF

97 NLFP APPT

Memo – Note

Prepared by – Établi par

Date

Overpayment – Paiement en trop
84

Balance due – Solde dû
86

Amount enclosed – Somme jointe

SIN of the proprietor(s) or principal owner(s) – NAS du ou des propriétaires

Canadian-controlled private corporations or unincorporated employers
Sociétés privées sous contrôle canadien ou employeurs non constitués
74 75

Person to contact about this return – Personne avec qui communiquer au sujet de cette déclaration
76

Area code / Indicatif régional
78

Telephone number / Numéro de téléphone

Extension / Poste

Certification – Attestation

I certify that the information given in this T4 return (T4 Summary and related T4 slips) is, to the best of my knowledge, correct and complete.
J'atteste que les renseignements fournis dans cette déclaration T4 (le formulaire T4 *Sommaire* et les feuillets T4 connexes) sont, à ma connaissance, exacts et complets.

Date

Signature of authorized person – Signature d'une personne autorisée

Position or office – Titre ou poste

Privacy Act, personal information bank number RCT/P-PU-005
Loi sur la protection des renseignements personnels, fichier de renseignements personnels numéro RCT/P-PU-005

T4 Summary – Sommaire (01)

Canada

NAME:______________________

Problem 13.6

Instruction 1

Employee	Weekly Pay	Wages Through October	Nov. 1–7 Taxable Wages for CPP	CPP Contribution	Nov. 1–7 Taxable Wages for EI	EI Premium
A	$880	$37,750	______	______	______	______
B	700	37,040	______	______	______	______
C	875	37,760	______	______	______	______
D	860	36,895	______	______	______	______
E	1,046	45,000	______	______	______	______
F	744	32,000	______	______	______	______
	Totals		______	______	______	______

Instruction 2

Employee	Weekly Pay	Cumulative Wages Through Nov. 7	Nov. 8–14 Taxable Wages for CPP	CPP Contribution	Nov. 8–14 Taxable Wages for EI	EI Premium
A	$880		______	______	______	______
B	700		______	______	______	______
C	875		______	______	______	______
D	860		______	______	______	______
E	1,046		______	______	______	______
F	744		______	______	______	______
	Totals		______	______	______	______

NAME:______________________________

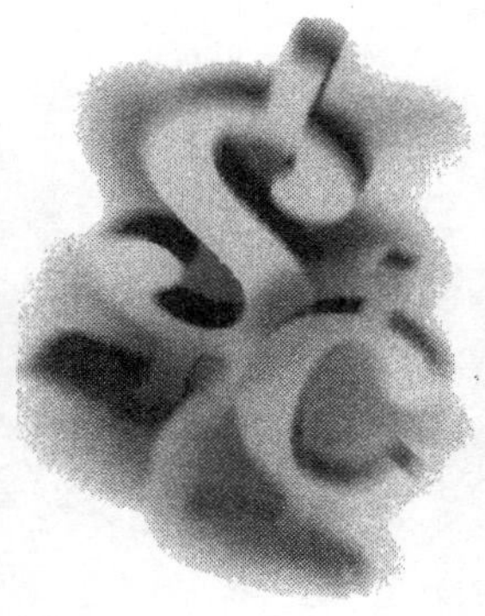

Comprehensive Problem 3

NAME:________________________

Comprehensive Problem 3

Instruction 2

PAYROLL REGISTER — **Week of December 4–8, 20XX**

Employee	Total Hours	Hourly Rate	Regular Earnings	Overtime Earnings	Gross Earnings	Fed'l Claim Code	Prov'l Claim Code	Deductions							Net Pay
								CPP Contributions	EI Premiums	Federal Income Tax	Provincial Income Tax	Union Dues	Charitable Contributions	Total Deductions	
Mathers															
Livingston															
Tomlin															
Tremblay															
Howard															
Totals															

NAME: ______________________

Comprehensive Problem 3 *(continued)*

Instruction 2

PAYROLL REGISTER																Week of December 11–15, 20XX
								Deductions								
Employee	Total Hours	Hourly Rate	Regular Earnings	Overtime Earnings	Gross Earnings	Fed'l Claim Code	Prov'l Claim Code	CPP Contributions	EI Premiums	Federal Income Tax	Provincial Income Tax	Union Dues	Charitable Contributions	Total Deductions	Net Pay	
Mathers																
Livingston																
Tomlin																
Tremblay*																
Howard																
Totals																

* Since Tremblay exceeds the maximum earnings of $38,300 for CPP, deduct an amount that will bring her total CPP contribution to $1,496.40.

NAME: ____________________

Comprehensive Problem 3 *(continued)*

Instruction 2

PAYROLL REGISTER																Week of December 18–22, 20XX
								Deductions								
Employee	Total Hours	Hourly Rate	Regular Earnings	Overtime Earnings	Gross Earnings	Fed'l Claim Code	Prov'l Claim Code	CPP Contributions	EI Premiums	Federal Income Tax	Provincial Income Tax	Union Dues	Charitable Contributions	Total Deductions	Net Pay	
Mathers																
Livingston																
Tomlin																
Tremblay																
Howard																
Totals																

NAME: ______________________________

Comprehensive Problem 3 *(continued)*

Instruction 2

PAYROLL REGISTER — **Week of December 25–29, 20XX**

								Deductions							
Employee	Total Hours	Hourly Rate	Regular Earnings	Overtime Earnings	Gross Earnings	Fed'l Claim Code	Prov'l Claim Code	CPP Contributions	EI Premiums	Federal Income Tax	Provincial Income Tax	Union Dues	Charitable Contributions	Total Deductions	Net Pay
Mathers															
Livingston															
Tomlin															
Tremblay															
Howard															
Totals															

Note: December 25 and 26 are paid holidays for all employees. Thus, each employee is paid for 40 hours' work.

NAME: ____________________

Comprehensive Problem 3 *(continued)*

Instruction 2

EMPLOYEE'S INDIVIDUAL EARNINGS RECORD

Name: Mathers, Doug Employee No.: 1 Date Employed: 11/3/19X1

Address: 1702 Wellington St., Owen Sound, Ont. L4R 3X9 Social Insurance No.: 304-628-917

Female: ____ Male: X Federal Net Claim Code: 2 Provincial Net Claim Code: 2

Married: X Single: ____ Pay Rate: $46,800 Per: Year

Phone No.: 123-4556 Date of Birth: 09/06/53

Period Ending	Gross Earnings	Deductions							Net Pay
		CPP Contributions	EI Premiums	Federal Income Tax	Provincial Income Tax	Union Dues	Charitable Contributions	Total Deductions	
Cumulative to Dec. 1	43 200 —	1 496 40	877 50	6 201 60	2 524 80		720 00	11 820 30	31 379 70

NAME: ____________________

Comprehensive Problem 3 *(continued)*

Instruction 2

EMPLOYEE'S INDIVIDUAL EARNINGS RECORD

Name: Livingston, Brenda — Employee No.: 2 — Date Employed: 1/5/19X2

Address: 42 Summerside Drive, Owen Sound, Ont. L4R 3X9 — Social Insurance No.: 406-281-755

Female: X — Male: ____ — Federal Net Claim Code: 1 — Provincial Net Claim Code: 1

Married: X — Single: ____ — Pay Rate: $20.00 — Per: Hour

Phone No.: 123-7852 — Date of Birth: 10/06/69

Period Ending	Gross Earnings	Deductions: CPP Contributions	Deductions: EI Premiums	Deductions: Federal Income Tax	Deductions: Provincial Income Tax	Deductions: Union Dues	Deductions: Charitable Contributions	Deductions: Total Deductions	Net Pay
Cumulative to Dec. 1	38 400 —	1 496 40	864 00	5 311 20	2 109 60	480 00		10 261 20	28 138 80

NAME: ____________________

Comprehensive Problem 3 *(continued)*

Instruction 2

EMPLOYEE'S INDIVIDUAL EARNINGS RECORD

Name: Tomlin, Scott **Employee No.:** 3 **Date Employed:** 2/7/19X3

Address: 324 Queen Street S., Owen Sound, Ont. L4R 3X7 **Social Insurance No.:** 409-672-815

Female: ____ **Male:** X **Federal Net Claim Code:** 3 **Provincial Net Claim Code:** 3

Married: ____ **Single:** X **Pay Rate:** $19.50 **Per:** Hour

Phone No.: 123-9003 **Date of Birth:** 07/28/74

Period Ending	Gross Earnings	Deductions							
		CPP Contributions	EI Premiums	Federal Income Tax	Provincial Income Tax	Union Dues	Charitable Contributions	Total Deductions	Net Pay
Cumulative to Dec. 1	37 440 —	1 462 24	842 39	4 934 40	1 900 80	480 00		9 619 83	27 820 17

Comprehensive Problem 3 *(continued)*

Instruction 2

EMPLOYEE'S INDIVIDUAL EARNINGS RECORD

Name: Tremblay, Jill **Employee No.:** 4 **Date Employed:** 5/4/19X3

Address: 3275 Dunedin Road, Meaford, Ont. L0L 1S4 **Social Insurance No.:** 503-287-152

Female: X **Male:** ____ **Federal Net Claim Code:** 2 **Provincial Net Claim Code:** 2

Married: X **Single:** ____ **Pay Rate:** $19.25 **Per:** Hour

Phone No.: 532-0129 **Date of Birth:** 04/23/72

Period Ending	Gross Earnings	Deductions							
		CPP Contributions	EI Premiums	Federal Income Tax	Provincial Income Tax	Union Dues	Charitable Contributions	Total Deductions	Net Pay
Cumulative to Dec. 1	36 960 —	1 441 18	831 61	4 850 40	1 956 00	480 00	480 00	10 039 19	26 920 81

NAME: ____________________

Comprehensive Problem 3 *(continued)*

Instruction 2

EMPLOYEE'S INDIVIDUAL EARNINGS RECORD

Name: Howard, Jan **Employee No.:** 5 **Date Employed:** 12/4/20XX

Address: 193 Highview Drive, Thornbury, Ont. L0L 2V0 **Social Insurance No.:** 208-113-564

Female: X **Male:** ____ **Federal Net Claim Code:** 1 **Provincial Net Claim Code:** 1

Married: ____ **Single:** X **Pay Rate:** $31,200 **Per:** Year

Phone No.: 428-1702 **Date of Birth:** 09/26/70

Period Ending	Gross Earnings	Deductions							
		CPP Contributions	EI Premiums	Federal Income Tax	Provincial Income Tax	Union Dues	Charitable Contributions	Total Deductions	Net Pay
Cumulative to Dec. 1									

NAME:____________________

Comprehensive Problem 3 *(continued)*

Instruction 3

GENERAL JOURNAL				PAGE NO.
Date	Description	Post. Ref.	Debit	Credit

NAME:____________________

Comprehensive Problem 3 *(continued)*

Instruction 3

GENERAL JOURNAL				PAGE NO.
Date	Description	Post. Ref.	Debit	Credit

NAME: ____________________

Comprehensive Problem 3 *(continued)*

Instruction 3

GENERAL JOURNAL **PAGE NO.**

Date		Description	Post. Ref.	Debit	Credit

NAME:______________________

Comprehensive Problem 3 *(continued)*

Instruction 3

GENERAL JOURNAL — **PAGE NO.**

Date	Description	Post. Ref.	Debit	Credit

NAME:____________________

Comprehensive Problem 3 *(continued)*

Instruction 4

GENERAL LEDGER

CASH — ACCT. NO. 101

Date		Explanation	Post. Ref.	Debit	Credit	Balance
20XX Dec.	1	Balance Forward	✓			2 5 0 4 4 35

WAGES PAYABLE — ACCT. NO. 205

Date		Explanation	Post. Ref.	Debit	Credit	Balance

NAME:________________________

Comprehensive Problem 3 *(continued)*

Instruction 4

CANADA PENSION PLAN PAYABLE **ACCT. NO. 210**

Date		Explanation	Post. Ref.	Debit	Credit	Balance
20XX Dec.	1	Balance Forward	✓			731 98

EMPLOYMENT INSURANCE PAYABLE **ACCT. NO. 215**

Date		Explanation	Post. Ref.	Debit	Credit	Balance
20XX Dec.	1	Balance Forward	✓			444 96

NAME:____________________

Comprehensive Problem 3 *(continued)*

Instruction 4

FEDERAL INCOME TAX PAYABLE — **ACCT. NO. 220**

Date 20XX		Explanation	Post. Ref.	Debit	Credit	Balance
Dec.	1	Balance Forward	✓			1 764 60

PROVINCIAL INCOME TAX PAYABLE — **ACCT. NO. 222**

Date 20XX		Explanation	Post. Ref.	Debit	Credit	Balance
Dec.	1	Balance Forward	✓			707 60

NAME:______________________

Comprehensive Problem 3 *(continued)*

Instruction 4

UNION DUES PAYABLE **ACCT. NO. 225**

Date		Explanation	Post. Ref.	Debit	Credit	Balance

CHARITABLE CONTRIBUTIONS PAYABLE **ACCT. NO. 240**

Date		Explanation	Post. Ref.	Debit	Credit	Balance

WAGES EXPENSE **ACCT. NO. 610**

Date		Explanation	Post. Ref.	Debit	Credit	Balance

NAME: ____________________

Comprehensive Problem 3 *(continued)*

Instruction 4

PAYROLL TAX EXPENSE **ACCT. NO. 615**

Date		Explanation	Post. Ref.	Debit	Credit	Balance

WORKERS' COMPENSATION INSURANCE EXPENSE **ACCT. NO. 620**

Date		Explanation	Post. Ref.	Debit	Credit	Balance

NAME:________________________

Comprehensive Problem 3 *(continued)* Instruction 5

Employer's name – Nom de l'employeur

Canada Customs and Revenue Agency / Agence des douanes et du revenu du Canada

T4

STATEMENT OF REMUNERATION PAID
ÉTAT DE LA RÉMUNÉRATION PAYÉE

Year / Année

VOID / ANNULÉ

14 Employment income – line 101 / Revenus d'emploi – ligne 101

22 Income tax deducted – line 437 / Impôt sur le revenu retenu – ligne 437

54 Business Number / Numéro d'entreprise

10 Province of employment / Province d'emploi

16 Employee's CPP contributions – line 308 / Cotisations de l'employé au RPC – ligne 308

24 EI insurable earnings / Gains assurables d'AE

12 Social insurance number / Numéro d'assurance sociale

28 Exempt – Exemption: CPP - QPP / RPC - RRQ; EI / AE

29 Employment Code / Code d'emploi

17 Employee's QPP contributions – line 308 / Cotisations de l'employé au RRQ – ligne 308

26 CPP-QPP pensionable earnings / Gains donnant droit à pension - RPC-RRQ

Employee's name and address – Nom et adresse de l'employé

Last name (in capital letters) – Nom de famille (en lettres majuscules) | First name – Prénom | Initials – Initiales

18 Employee's EI premiums – line 312 / Cotisations de l'employé à l'AE – ligne 312

44 Union dues – line 212 / Cotisations syndicales – ligne 212

20 RPP contributions – line 207 / Cotisations à un RPA – ligne 207

46 Charitable donations – Schedule 1 / Dons de bienfaisance – Annexe 1

52 Pension adjustment – line 206 / Facteur d'équivalence – ligne 206

50 RPP or DPSP registration number / N° d'agrément d'un RPA ou d'un RPDB

Other information (see the back) / Autres renseignements (voir au verso)

Box – Case | Amount – Montant | Box – Case | Amount – Montant

Box – Case | Amount – Montant | Box – Case | Amount – Montant | Box – Case | Amount – Montant | Box – Case | Amount – Montant

T4 (01)

Employer's name – Nom de l'employeur

Canada Customs and Revenue Agency / Agence des douanes et du revenu du Canada

T4

STATEMENT OF REMUNERATION PAID
ÉTAT DE LA RÉMUNÉRATION PAYÉE

Year / Année

VOID / ANNULÉ

14 Employment income – line 101 / Revenus d'emploi – ligne 101

22 Income tax deducted – line 437 / Impôt sur le revenu retenu – ligne 437

54 Business Number / Numéro d'entreprise

10 Province of employment / Province d'emploi

16 Employee's CPP contributions – line 308 / Cotisations de l'employé au RPC – ligne 308

24 EI insurable earnings / Gains assurables d'AE

12 Social insurance number / Numéro d'assurance sociale

28 Exempt – Exemption: CPP - QPP / RPC - RRQ; EI / AE

29 Employment Code / Code d'emploi

17 Employee's QPP contributions – line 308 / Cotisations de l'employé au RRQ – ligne 308

26 CPP-QPP pensionable earnings / Gains donnant droit à pension - RPC-RRQ

Employee's name and address – Nom et adresse de l'employé

Last name (in capital letters) – Nom de famille (en lettres majuscules) | First name – Prénom | Initials – Initiales

18 Employee's EI premiums – line 312 / Cotisations de l'employé à l'AE – ligne 312

44 Union dues – line 212 / Cotisations syndicales – ligne 212

20 RPP contributions – line 207 / Cotisations à un RPA – ligne 207

46 Charitable donations – Schedule 1 / Dons de bienfaisance – Annexe 1

52 Pension adjustment – line 206 / Facteur d'équivalence – ligne 206

50 RPP or DPSP registration number / N° d'agrément d'un RPA ou d'un RPDB

Other information (see the back) / Autres renseignements (voir au verso)

Box – Case | Amount – Montant | Box – Case | Amount – Montant

Box – Case | Amount – Montant | Box – Case | Amount – Montant | Box – Case | Amount – Montant | Box – Case | Amount – Montant

T4 (01)

NAME: ______________________________

Comprehensive Problem 3 *(continued)* Instruction 5

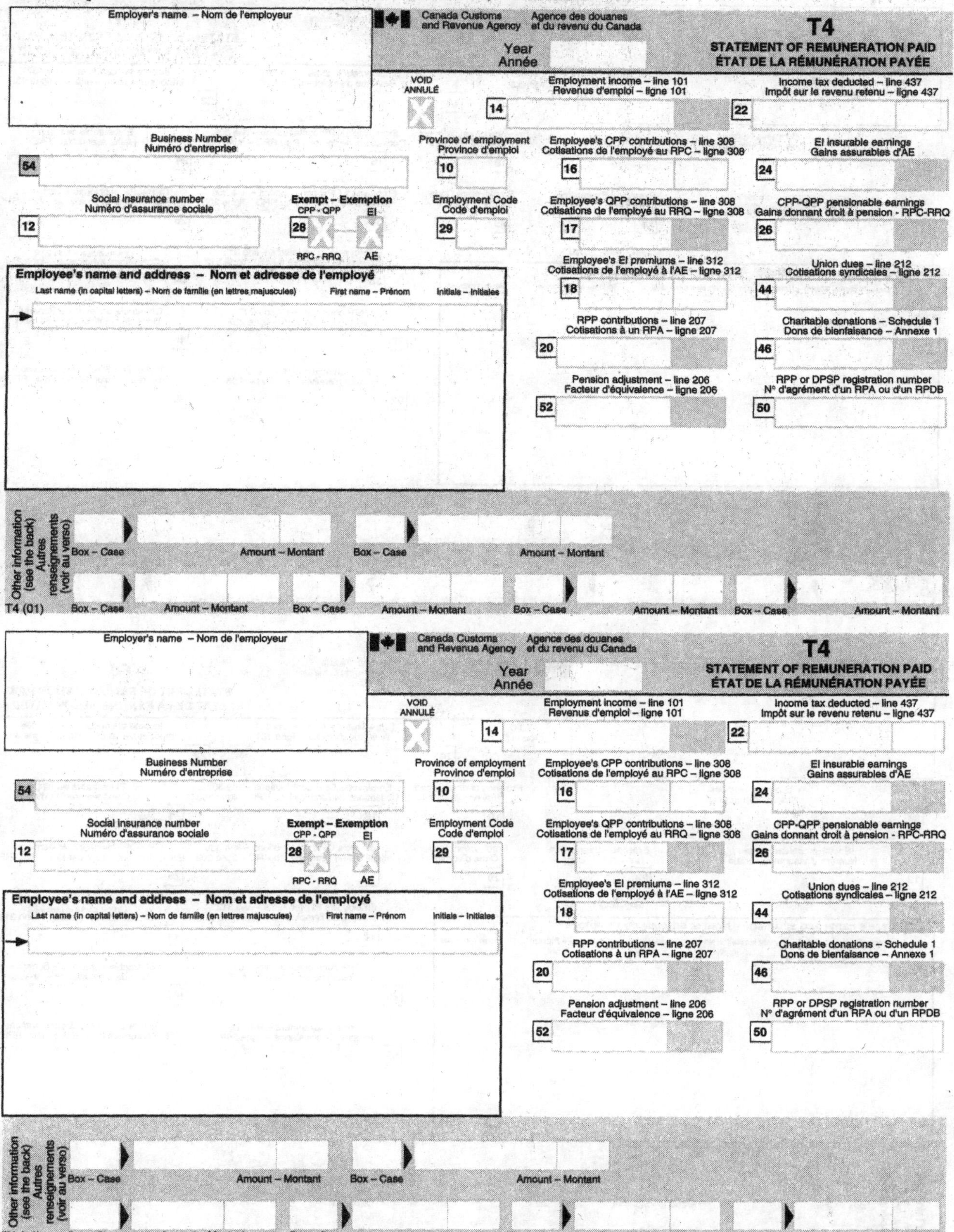

Employer's name – Nom de l'employeur

Canada Customs and Revenue Agency — Agence des douanes et du revenu du Canada

Year / Année

T4
STATEMENT OF REMUNERATION PAID
ÉTAT DE LA RÉMUNÉRATION PAYÉE

VOID / ANNULÉ

14 Employment income – line 101 / Revenus d'emploi – ligne 101

22 Income tax deducted – line 437 / Impôt sur le revenu retenu – ligne 437

54 Business Number / Numéro d'entreprise

10 Province of employment / Province d'emploi

16 Employee's CPP contributions – line 308 / Cotisations de l'employé au RPC – ligne 308

24 EI insurable earnings / Gains assurables d'AE

12 Social insurance number / Numéro d'assurance sociale

28 Exempt – Exemption: CPP - QPP / RPC - RRQ; EI / AE

29 Employment Code / Code d'emploi

17 Employee's QPP contributions – line 308 / Cotisations de l'employé au RRQ – ligne 308

26 CPP-QPP pensionable earnings / Gains donnant droit à pension - RPC-RRQ

Employee's name and address – Nom et adresse de l'employé

Last name (in capital letters) – Nom de famille (en lettres majuscules) | First name – Prénom | Initials – Initiales

18 Employee's EI premiums – line 312 / Cotisations de l'employé à l'AE – ligne 312

44 Union dues – line 212 / Cotisations syndicales – ligne 212

20 RPP contributions – line 207 / Cotisations à un RPA – ligne 207

46 Charitable donations – Schedule 1 / Dons de bienfaisance – Annexe 1

52 Pension adjustment – line 206 / Facteur d'équivalence – ligne 206

50 RPP or DPSP registration number / N° d'agrément d'un RPA ou d'un RPDB

Other information (see the back) / Autres renseignements (voir au verso)

Box – Case | Amount – Montant | Box – Case | Amount – Montant

Box – Case | Amount – Montant | Box – Case | Amount – Montant | Box – Case | Amount – Montant | Box – Case | Amount – Montant

T4 (01)

Employer's name – Nom de l'employeur

Canada Customs and Revenue Agency — Agence des douanes et du revenu du Canada

Year / Année

T4
STATEMENT OF REMUNERATION PAID
ÉTAT DE LA RÉMUNÉRATION PAYÉE

VOID / ANNULÉ

14 Employment income – line 101 / Revenus d'emploi – ligne 101

22 Income tax deducted – line 437 / Impôt sur le revenu retenu – ligne 437

54 Business Number / Numéro d'entreprise

10 Province of employment / Province d'emploi

16 Employee's CPP contributions – line 308 / Cotisations de l'employé au RPC – ligne 308

24 EI insurable earnings / Gains assurables d'AE

12 Social insurance number / Numéro d'assurance sociale

28 Exempt – Exemption: CPP - QPP / RPC - RRQ; EI / AE

29 Employment Code / Code d'emploi

17 Employee's QPP contributions – line 308 / Cotisations de l'employé au RRQ – ligne 308

26 CPP-QPP pensionable earnings / Gains donnant droit à pension - RPC-RRQ

Employee's name and address – Nom et adresse de l'employé

Last name (in capital letters) – Nom de famille (en lettres majuscules) | First name – Prénom | Initials – Initiales

18 Employee's EI premiums – line 312 / Cotisations de l'employé à l'AE – ligne 312

44 Union dues – line 212 / Cotisations syndicales – ligne 212

20 RPP contributions – line 207 / Cotisations à un RPA – ligne 207

46 Charitable donations – Schedule 1 / Dons de bienfaisance – Annexe 1

52 Pension adjustment – line 206 / Facteur d'équivalence – ligne 206

50 RPP or DPSP registration number / N° d'agrément d'un RPA ou d'un RPDB

Other information (see the back) / Autres renseignements (voir au verso)

Box – Case | Amount – Montant | Box – Case | Amount – Montant

Box – Case | Amount – Montant | Box – Case | Amount – Montant | Box – Case | Amount – Montant | Box – Case | Amount – Montant

T4 (01)

NAME: ____________________

Comprehensive Problem 3 *(continued)* Instruction 5

Employer's name – Nom de l'employeur

Canada Customs and Revenue Agency / Agence des douanes et du revenu du Canada

T4

STATEMENT OF REMUNERATION PAID
ÉTAT DE LA RÉMUNÉRATION PAYÉE

Year / Année

VOID / ANNULÉ

14 Employment income – line 101 / Revenus d'emploi – ligne 101

22 Income tax deducted – line 437 / Impôt sur le revenu retenu – ligne 437

54 Business Number / Numéro d'entreprise

10 Province of employment / Province d'emploi

16 Employee's CPP contributions – line 308 / Cotisations de l'employé au RPC – ligne 308

24 EI insurable earnings / Gains assurables d'AE

12 Social insurance number / Numéro d'assurance sociale

28 Exempt – Exemption: CPP - QPP / RPC - RRQ; EI / AE

29 Employment Code / Code d'emploi

17 Employee's QPP contributions – line 308 / Cotisations de l'employé au RRQ – ligne 308

26 CPP-QPP pensionable earnings / Gains donnant droit à pension - RPC-RRQ

Employee's name and address – Nom et adresse de l'employé

Last name (in capital letters) – Nom de famille (en lettres majuscules) | First name – Prénom | Initials – Initiales

18 Employee's EI premiums – line 312 / Cotisations de l'employé à l'AE – ligne 312

44 Union dues – line 212 / Cotisations syndicales – ligne 212

20 RPP contributions – line 207 / Cotisations à un RPA – ligne 207

46 Charitable donations – Schedule 1 / Dons de bienfaisance – Annexe 1

52 Pension adjustment – line 206 / Facteur d'équivalence – ligne 206

50 RPP or DPSP registration number / N° d'agrément d'un RPA ou d'un RPDB

Other information (see the back) / Autres renseignements (voir au verso)

Box – Case | Amount – Montant | Box – Case | Amount – Montant

Box – Case | Amount – Montant | Box – Case | Amount – Montant | Box – Case | Amount – Montant | Box – Case | Amount – Montant

T4 (01)

Employer's name – Nom de l'employeur

Canada Customs and Revenue Agency / Agence des douanes et du revenu du Canada

T4

STATEMENT OF REMUNERATION PAID
ÉTAT DE LA RÉMUNÉRATION PAYÉE

Year / Année

VOID / ANNULÉ

14 Employment income – line 101 / Revenus d'emploi – ligne 101

22 Income tax deducted – line 437 / Impôt sur le revenu retenu – ligne 437

54 Business Number / Numéro d'entreprise

10 Province of employment / Province d'emploi

16 Employee's CPP contributions – line 308 / Cotisations de l'employé au RPC – ligne 308

24 EI insurable earnings / Gains assurables d'AE

12 Social insurance number / Numéro d'assurance sociale

28 Exempt – Exemption: CPP - QPP / RPC - RRQ; EI / AE

29 Employment Code / Code d'emploi

17 Employee's QPP contributions – line 308 / Cotisations de l'employé au RRQ – ligne 308

26 CPP-QPP pensionable earnings / Gains donnant droit à pension - RPC-RRQ

Employee's name and address – Nom et adresse de l'employé

Last name (in capital letters) – Nom de famille (en lettres majuscules) | First name – Prénom | Initials – Initiales

18 Employee's EI premiums – line 312 / Cotisations de l'employé à l'AE – ligne 312

44 Union dues – line 212 / Cotisations syndicales – ligne 212

20 RPP contributions – line 207 / Cotisations à un RPA – ligne 207

46 Charitable donations – Schedule 1 / Dons de bienfaisance – Annexe 1

52 Pension adjustment – line 206 / Facteur d'équivalence – ligne 206

50 RPP or DPSP registration number / N° d'agrément d'un RPA ou d'un RPDB

Other information (see the back) / Autres renseignements (voir au verso)

Box – Case | Amount – Montant | Box – Case | Amount – Montant

Box – Case | Amount – Montant | Box – Case | Amount – Montant | Box – Case | Amount – Montant | Box – Case | Amount – Montant

T4 (01)

Comprehensive Problem 3 *(continued)*

NAME: ______________________

Instruction 6

Canada Customs and Revenue Agency / Agence des douanes et du revenu du Canada

For the year ending December 31, / Pour l'année se terminant le 31 décembre 20____

Web Access Code – Code d'accès au Web

0505 **T4** Summary / Sommaire

SUMMARY OF REMUNERATION PAID
SOMMAIRE DE LA RÉMUNÉRATION PAYÉE

You have to file your T 4 return on or before the last day of **February**.
See the information on the back of this form.

Vous devez produire votre déclaration T4 au plus tard le dernier jour de **février**.
Lisez les renseignements au verso de ce formulaire.

Business Number – Numéro d'entreprise

Name and address of employer – Nom et adresse de l'employeur

Total number of T4 slips filed – Nombre total de feuillets T4 produits 88

Employment income – Revenus d'emploi 14

Registered pension plan (RPP) contributions
Cotisations à un régime de pension agréé (RPA) 20

Pension adjustment – Facteur d'équivalence 52

Indicate how many T4 slips are for employees whose addresses are in the U.S.A.

Indiquez le nombre de feuillets T4 émis pour des employés dont l'adresse est aux États-Unis.

Employee's CPP contributions – Cotisations de l'employé au RPC 16

Employer's CPP contributions – Cotisations de l'employeur au RPC 27

Employee's EI premiums – Cotisations de l'employé à l'AE 18

Employer's EI premiums – Cotisations de l'employeur à l'AE 19

Income tax deducted – Impôt sur le revenu retenu 22

Total deductions reported (16 + 27 + 18 + 19 + 22)
Total des retenues déclarées (16 + 27 + 18 + 19 + 22) 80

Minus: remittances – Moins : versements 82

We do not charge or refund a difference of less than $2.

Nous n'exigeons ni ne remboursons une différence inférieure à 2 $.

Difference – Différence

Do not use this area – N'inscrivez rien ici

90 Last to current / Précédente à courante 1 2 Other / Autre 3

91 Pro Forma 1 2

93 Y – A D – J

94 PD15-1

96 POF PSF

97 NLFP APPT

Memo – Note

Prepared by – Établi par

Date

Overpayment – Paiement en trop 84

Balance due – Solde dû 86

Amount enclosed – Somme jointe

Canadian-controlled private corporations or unincorporated employers
Sociétés privées sous contrôle canadien ou employeurs non constitués

SIN of the proprietor(s) or principal owner(s) – NAS du ou des propriétaires 74 75

Person to contact about this return – Personne avec qui communiquer au sujet de cette déclaration 76

Area code / Indicatif régional 78

Telephone number / Numéro de téléphone

Extension / Poste

Certification – Attestation

I certify that the information given in this T4 return (T4 Summary and related T4 slips) is, to the best of my knowledge, correct and complete.
J'atteste que les renseignements fournis dans cette déclaration T4 (le formulaire T4 *Sommaire* et les feuillets T4 connexes) sont, à ma connaissance, exacts et complets.

Date

Signature of authorized person – Signature d'une personne autorisée

Position or office – Titre ou poste

Privacy Act, personal information bank number RCT/P-PU-005
Loi sur la protection des renseignements personnels, fichier de renseignements personnels numéro RCT/P-PU-005

T4 Summary – Sommaire (01)

Canada

NAME:______________________

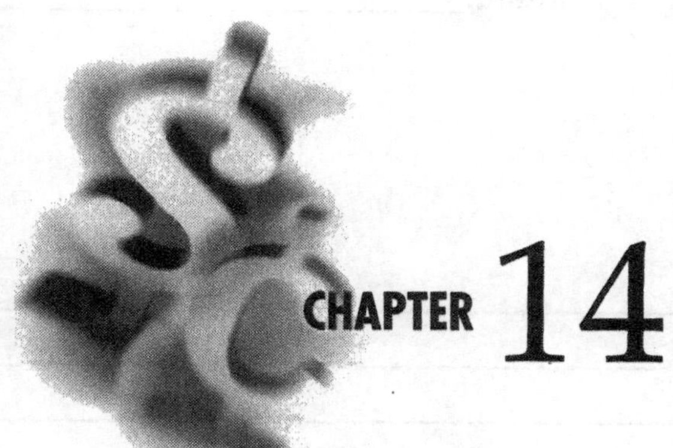

CHAPTER 14

Partnership Accounting

Vocabulary Review

1. ______________________
2. ______________________
3. ______________________
4. ______________________
5. ______________________
6. ______________________
7. ______________________
8. ______________________
9. ______________________
10. ______________________
11. ______________________
12. ______________________
13. ______________________
14. ______________________
15. ______________________
16. ______________________

NAME: ______________________

Exercise 14.1

a. ______________________

b. ______________________

____

____

____

c.

	Morton	Long	Total
Amount to be divided			

NAME:________________________

Exercise 14.2

	Morton	Long	Total
Amount to be divided			

NAME:________________________

Exercise 14.3

GENERAL JOURNAL				PAGE NO.	
Date		Description	Post. Ref.	Debit	Credit

NAME:____________________

Exercise 14.4

GENERAL JOURNAL PAGE NO.

Date		Description	Post. Ref.	Debit	Credit

NAME:________________________

Exercise 14.5

GENERAL JOURNAL				PAGE NO.
Date	Description	Post. Ref.	Debit	Credit

NAME:________________________

Exercise 14.5 *(continued)*

GENERAL JOURNAL				PAGE NO.
Date	Description	Post. Ref.	Debit	Credit

NAME:______________________

Exercise 14.6

a.

b.

c.

Martin will receive cash of $________

Pearson will receive cash of $________

Henderson will receive cash of $________

NAME:______________________

Exercise 14.7

a. ______________________

____

b. ______________________

____

____

____

____

____

c. (1) Baker will receive cash of $______

Marshall will receive cash of $______

Perryman will receive cash of $______

(2) ______________________

Baker will receive cash of $______

Marshall will receive cash of $______

Perryman will receive cash of $______

NAME:________________________

Problem 14.1

a.

Plan	Calculations	Jones	Brady	Bell	Total Allocated

NAME:___________________

Problem 14.1 *(continued)*

b.

____

____

____

Net income		
Allocation of Net Income to partners:		
Jones		
Brady		
Bell		
Total Net Income allocated		

NAME:______________________________

Problem 14.1 *(continued)*

c.

GENERAL JOURNAL				PAGE NO.	
Date		Description	Post. Ref.	Debit	Credit

NAME:____________________

Problem 14.2

GENERAL JOURNAL | **PAGE NO.**

Date		Description	Post. Ref.	Debit	Credit

NAME:________________________

Problem 14.3

GENERAL JOURNAL			PAGE NO.	
Date	Description	Post. Ref.	Debit	Credit

a.

c.

NAME:________________________

Problem 14.3 *(continued)*

b.

Calculations	Coleman	Simmons	Total Allocated

NAME:______________________________

Problem 14.3 *(continued)*

d.

____

____

____

NAME:________________________

Problem 14.3 *(continued)*

e.

____

____

____

	Coleman	Simmons	Total

Problem 14.3 *(continued)*

f.

____

____

____

NAME:________________________

Problem 14.4

GENERAL JOURNAL PAGE NO.

Date		Description	Post. Ref.	Debit	Credit

NAME:________________________

Problem 14.5

GENERAL JOURNAL			PAGE NO.	
Date	Description	Post. Ref.	Debit	Credit

NAME: ______________________

Problem 14.6

GENERAL JOURNAL PAGE NO.

Date		Description	Post. Ref.	Debit	Credit

NAME:______________________________

Problem 14.6 *(continued)*

GENERAL JOURNAL PAGE NO.

Date		Description	Post. Ref.	Debit	Credit

NAME: ____________________

Problem 14.7

GENERAL JOURNAL			PAGE NO.	
Date	Description	Post. Ref.	Debit	Credit

NAME:________________________

Problem 14.7 *(continued)*

GENERAL JOURNAL PAGE NO.

Date		Description	Post. Ref.	Debit	Credit

NAME:________________________

Problem 14.7 *(continued)*

GENERAL JOURNAL				PAGE NO.	
Date		Description	Post. Ref.	Debit	Credit

NOTES

NOTES

NOTES

NOTES

NOTES